THE BOOK OF DANIEL

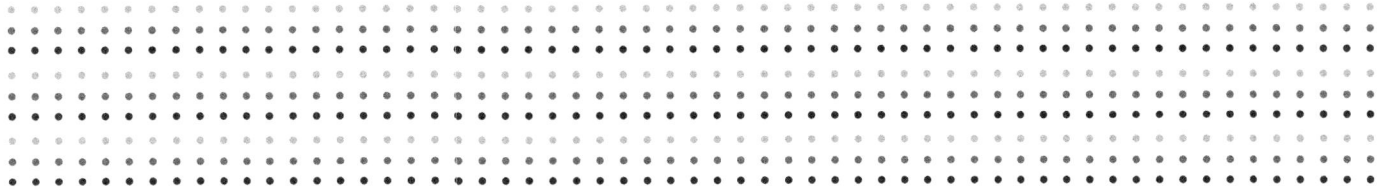

A Verse By Verse Commentary
Prof. Tom Meyer

To Pat:
You have been such a tremendous blessing in my life.
Your love for God and his Word is undeniable.
Thank you for often enriching me with certainties and uncertainties.
Keep praying for us as we do our best to "walk in truth."
We love and appreciate you.

Table of Contents

Introduction

The book of Daniel is a verse by verse commentary on one of the greatest prophetic books of the Old Testament, written and edited by Prof. Tom Meyer. It attempts to treat the book on a verse by verse basis seen through a Middle Eastern cultural lens with an emphasis on geography, culture, history and archeology. I have presented the results of my own careful, personal Bible study and lengthy exposure of living in the Land of the Bible for 1,000 days. I also have some of Daniel memorized and feel I have great contributions and insights to offer the Bible student. For the convenience of the reader, the King James Version is used; all Biblical phraseology appears in bold face type, as do all the Biblical verse numbers. The commentary is therefore, strictly speaking, neither a devotional nor a technical exegetical treatment. It seeks to present the messages of the book of Daniel in such a way that the Bible student, whether a novice or serious will find extensive explanation, illumination and clarification within its pages.

Daniel 1

[1] In the third year of the reign of Jehoiakim king of Judah came Nebuchadnezzar king of Babylon unto Jerusalem, and besieged it.

The first two verses introduce not only the opening chapter but the entire book and give a historical framework for some of the most awful events in the history of Judah. They also give us a historical, chronological, geographical, and theological lens through which to read the remainder of the book. King Jehoiakim was born in 634 BC and was the son of the famous godly king Josiah who was killed in action by an Egyptian archer at Megiddo (2 Chronicles 36:22), in the midst of the battle of Haran. His name was changed from Eliakim to Jehoiakim (YHWH has established) by Pharaoh-Neco around 624 BC when the Pharaoh deposed his brother Jehoahaz, and established Jehoiakim on the throne. This is the same evil king who in December of 604 BC cut into pieces and threw into the fire a scroll containing the prophecy of the 70 year captivity under Babylon from the mouth of Jeremiah (Jeremiah 36:9-32). The Egyptian army seized upon the floundering kingdom of Judah after the battle and exacted a heavy taxation of silver and gold from the people of the land in order to deposit it into the bank account of the Egyptian government (2 Kings 24:35). Jehoiakim's son was Jeconiah upon whom Jeremiah (23:30) pronounced the infamous curse that no man of his seed, that is a Son of David, will ever sit upon the throne of David to rule from Jerusalem anymore. Because of the curse, Jeconiah lost both land and family and was essentially "dead" in the worldview of the Ancient Near East. So if a Son of David cannot sit on the throne, how can Jesus, the Son of David, qualify for kingship? By being adopted by Joseph, Jesus is legally identified as a Son of David through his father's line, but because Jesus is not Joseph's biological son, he avoids the curse on Jeconiah's seed.

The first of the three waves of deportation of the inhabitants of Judah to Babylon occurred in 605 BC. This first wave included capturing not only the ruling elite in bonds (2 Chronicles 36: 5-6), but also the vessels of the house of God and the choice young men. The second wave of deportation occurred in 597 BC and included King Jehoiachin (whose evil father Jehoiakim had surrendered to Babylon and died in Israel: 2 Kings 24:6), and the religious elite, which included the prophet Ezekiel (2 Kings 24:11-16). The third and final deportation in connection with the destruction of the Jerusalem Temple occurred in 586 BC and included the de facto king Zedekiah and all the remaining able-body prisoners of war. The only Israelites left in the land were the "people of the land," the peasants who would till and work the land and livestock for the needs of the Babylonian Empire (2 Kings 25:12). Nebuchadnezzar, whose name means Nabu, god of Babylon, protect the borders, began his reign of 43 years in 605 BC. Babylon was considered by the Chaldeans to be the "jewel of kingdoms and the glory of the Babylonian's pride" (Isaiah 13:19). His father, Nabopolassar, was the founder of the Neo-Babylon Empire of the 7th and 6th centuries BC and reigned 21 years, from 626-605 BC. The first official year of a Babylonian king's reign coincided with the New Year holiday event (Akitu). The crowning ceremony also included political pardons around early April (2 Kings 25:27). The captives were taken to Babylon (Bab-ili), which in the Akkadian tongues meant Gate of the gods.

[2] And the Lord gave Jehoiakim king of Judah into his hand, with part of the vessels of the house of God: which he carried into the land of Shinar to the house of his god; and he brought the vessels into the treasure house of his god.

Adonai inflicted punishment on his rebellious people Judah by a nation less righteous than they, namely, Babylon. This point is made by the author, stating that "the Lord gave Judah into his (Nebuchadnezzar's) hand." The Hebrew word *yad*, which means hand, is often used figuratively to describe the authority or power of a deity or man. It was common for all temples in the Ancient Near East to have a designated space for sacred religious objects which are the property of the deity worshiped there. The Temple in Jerusalem had such designated storage areas (1 Chron. 9:26, 2 Chron. 31:11, Neh. 10:38). Nebuchadnezzar, following the standard *modus operandi* of the ANE brought the conquered Temple treasures (2 Kings 25:8-21) as trophies of war to Babylon and stored them in the temple of Belus alongside the vessels that were appointed to the idolatrous worship of Marduk, etc. Only the vessels were taken from the Temple and not an image of the God of Israel because of his being invisible. This abduction of the temple properties was prophesied long ago in the reign of Hezekiah by Isaiah (Isaiah 39:6). The total number of objects removed from the Temple Mount and brought to Babylon were 5,400 (Ezra 1:11). Esagila was the proper name of the magnificent temple of Marduk in Babylon where the objects were put on display and stored (Ezra 5:14). Marduk was the nation's prime deity but his popular name was Bel which means lord (Isaiah 46:1). Notice that not all, but part of the vessels were taken. Jeremiah states that a prominent number of objects, possibly including the hidden Ark of the Covenant, were still in Jerusalem after the first siege (Jeremiah 27:16-22). The removal of precious religious objects related to the defeated people's deity was to both physically and symbolically demonstrate the superiority of the victor's deity (1 Samuel 5:2). As Chemosh, the god of Moab, physically went into exile with the people of Moab along with the ruling elite (Jeremiah 38:7), so YHWH symbolically goes into exile with his people by having his glory depart from the Temple to east (Ezekiel 11:23).

The archaic term *Shinar* is first mentioned in the Table of Nations in Genesis chapter 10. The region of Shinar was ruled and reigned over originally by the infamous Nimrod. This should be considered the first empire in the post-flood world and the epicenter of false worship. The region was considered among the Hebrew prophets as a "dwelling of iniquity and wickedness" (Zechariah 5:5-11). The wife of Nimrod, Semiramas, was the first or one of the first women to be worshiped in a hypo-static fashion. In this region Nimrod built four cities of great importance, Babel (the Greek translation of Babel is Babylon), Erech, Accad, and Calneh in the land of Shinar. The land of Shinar is next mentioned in connection with the narrative of the open rebellion at the Tower of Babel. It is as if the author of Daniel is reminding us that this is the land where the chosen nation came from via their father Abram, but are now exiled from the land of promise to return to the land of confusion. Later in the rabbinic period the Talmud devises to answer why the Jews went into exile in Babylon rather than any other land. They said it was "because the home of Abraham was there. They tell a parable. Unto what is the matter like? It is like a woman who disgraces her husband so that he sends her away. He sends her away to the home of her father." In regards to idol worship the archeological record indicates that Israel learned their lesson in terms of worshiping foreign gods. There is scant if any evidences of idols found in the strata from the Persian period to the Roman period in Israel.

[3] And the king spake unto Ashpenaz the master of his eunuchs, that he should bring certain of the children of Israel, and of the king's seed, and of the princes;

Ashpenaz was the chief eunuch in the court of Nebuchadnezzar. His name means something like "horse's nose" or "I will make prominent the sprinkled." Some have suggested that his name is derived from an Old Persian word meaning 'innkeeper' which fits nicely with the narrative. The chief eunuch and those under him were likely castrated. This was the common custom of Oriental monarchs for those in positions of authority as superintendent over the care of the house of the women and other offices of the court. In regards to their position over the house of the women the procedure was evidently a precautionary measure to prevent the man from violating the king's harem. Ashpenaz would have handpicked the selection of these young men and been the overseer of their Babylonian education.

Interestingly the word *Israel* does not appear in the Aramaic section of Daniel, but does appear in the Hebrew section of Daniel in chapter nine (9:7, 11, 20). How were Daniel, Hananiah, Mishael, and Azariah of the royal family or nobility? The Scriptures do not inform us. Josephus claims that the young men were related to King Zedekiah and the church historian Jerome relates that they were related to King Hezekiah. Regardless, these four young men, along with countless others now captive in Babylon, would have likely had diplomatic and ambassadorial training in Jerusalem and could be further prepped for any future political correspondence needed between Jerusalem and Babylon. Over 100 years before this Isaiah prophesied that because of Hezekiah's folly the Babylonian captivity would occur and the sons of Judah would become eunuchs in the palace of the king of Babylon (Isaiah 39:7).

[4] Children in whom was no blemish, but well favoured, and skilful in all wisdom, and cunning in knowledge, and understanding science, and such as had ability in them to stand in the king's palace, and whom they might teach the learning and the tongue of the Chaldeans.

The prerequisites for serving in the palace of Babylon were the proper age, genealogy, physical appearance, intellect, and palace etiquette. The giftedness of the young men is closely related to the God given ability of Bezaleel the son of Uri, the son of Hur to devise the curious works for the Tabernacle (Exodus 35:31). As Moses excelled in the wisdom of Egypt, so these boys were dedicated to the same excellence in education. Both Bezaleel and the young men are skilful in wisdom, knowledge, and understanding. If indeed Daniel and the other young men were unwittingly forced to become eunuchs in the traditional sense of the term, they were not so in Israel as they are defined here as having no blemish. Diverse regulations in regards to Jewish temple rituals required that any male who was wounded in the stones or had his private member cut off could not enter into the congregation of the Lord (Deuteronomy 23:1). Also the term of having no blemish described the sons of Aaron who offered offerings (Leviticus 21:21) as well as the sacrifices that were offered (Numbers 19:2). Babylonian diviners were also held to similar regulations when they approached their deities.

The Hebrew captives would be indoctrinated in the learning and tongue of the Chaldeans. The terms *Chaldeans* and *Babylonians* are used interchangeably throughout the Scriptures. The language of the Babylonians would have primarily been Akkadian. Akkadian was a Semitic language frequently fashioned in wedged shaped letters on impressionable objects such as clay tablets. Their curriculum would have also included knowledge of the Sumerian tongue, the ecclesiological language of Babylon, and a mastery of the Aramaic tongue, the *lingua franca* or international trade language of the Fertile Crescent.

[5] And the king appointed them a daily provision of the king's meat, and of the wine which he drank: so nourishing them three years, that at the end thereof they might stand before the king.

This would have been a true culture shock for these kosher young men. The kings of Babylon were noted for their opulence and lifestyles of the rich and famous. The ancient Persian kings followed the custom of the Babylonian kings, and fed their entourage, both foreign and domestic, from their own tables (1 Kings 4:22-23). The Hebrew word for meat is *patbag* and is followed by the noun *hamelek* which means *the king*. This underlines the fact that this food came from the king's expense. This was no ordinary food but royal delicatessens on which the young men supped. Some suggest that a three-year education was standard practice in the Babylonian and Persian courts. Nevertheless, at the end of this duration the young men were submitted to an oral and physical exam including an interview with the king himself to determine if they would be introduced into royal service.

[6] Now among these were of the children of Judah, Daniel, Hananiah, Mishael, and Azariah:

Among the multitudes of young men meeting the above qualifications from the diverse nations which

Babylonian conquered in the Fertile Crescent region were some from Judah. These young men are part and parcel of the fulfilled prophecy spoken by Isaiah the prophet to King Hezekiah some 100 years before the first wave of Babylonian captivity. Because of Hezekiah's geopolitical affinity with Babylon and his exposing of the most precious things of the Temple of God to the Babylonian emissaries, a deportation was predicted which included "thy sons that shall issue from thee, which thou shalt beget, shall they take away, and they shall be eunuchs in the palace of the king of Babylon" (2 Kings 20:18).

Names in the world of the Bible were pregnant with expectations and the desires of their parents. There is no exception here as each of the young men have a theophoric name, that is, within their given name is a form of a divine name of God, whether Elohim or YHWH. Daniel means "Elohim's judge," which means one who delivers judgment in the name of Elohim. Hananiah means "whom YHWH gave," Mishael means "who is what Elohim is," and Azariah means "whom YHWH helps."

[7] Unto whom the prince of the eunuchs gave names: for he gave unto Daniel the name of Belteshazzar; and to Hananiah, of Shadrach; and to Mishael, of Meshach; and to Azariah, of Abed-nego.

In order to redefine the identity of the young Judean men the Babylonian monarchy prescribes for them a new name and hence a new character. In part, this is done to condition these young Hebrews into the thought and practice of the Babylonian religion and government and to cut off any existing ties to their home religion and government. Daniel's new name means "Bel's prince" or the prince whom Bel favors. This is a Babylonian theophoric name containing a form of the chief god Marduk who is also known as Bel. Later in Daniel 4:8 the aged wife of Nebuchadnezzar attests that Daniel was given his Babylonian name in honor of Nebuchadnezzar's chief deity. Hananiah's new name means something like "the great scribe." Mishael's new name means "guest of the king." Finally, Azariah's new name means "worshiper of Nebo." This is also a Babylonian theophoric name containing a form of Nebo, the god of wisdom and writing and the son of Marduk. Each of their new names now extols a pagan god.

[8] But Daniel purposed in his heart that he would not defile himself with the portion of the king's meat, nor with the wine which he drank: therefore he requested of the prince of the eunuchs that he might not defile himself.

Daniel along with all other Hebrews identified the heart as being the inner control center of the person. In a figurative sense, the heart is mentioned over 800 times in the Scriptures. Out of it flow all the issues of life (Proverbs 4:23), and it is the location of human character (Luke 6:45). Therefore, it is the aspect of man about which God is most concerned (1 Samuel 16:7). To the ancient Hebrews the heart served as the seat of all the spiritual, moral, intellectual, volitional and emotional aspects of a man's life. There was no geographical distance between the heart and the mind. There are at least two proposals as to why these young men chose to abstain from the royal diet. First and the most obvious is that the Mosaic Law did not permit the young men to consume the foodstuffs provided to them by the monarchy. Secondly, by eating with the pagan monarchy they would have been instilled with a sense of loyalty and allegiance to the Babylonian monarchy's culture and mannerisms.

[9] Now God had brought Daniel into favour and tender love with the prince of the eunuchs.

The duration of time the young men have been enrolled in the learning and tongue of the Chaldeans up to this point of controversy is not given. Nevertheless, the text conveys the notion that Daniel has proven his merit to the prince of the eunuchs. The reader is again reminded that in the midst of captivity God was in full control of the events at hand. A literary connection may be drawn here between Daniel and others in exile. The same concept of obtaining mercy or "favor" in captivity from the masters of the Hebrews is also found in the accounts of Joseph (Genesis 39:21), Ezra (Ezra 7:28), and Nehemiah (Nehemiah 2:8).

[10] And the prince of the eunuchs said unto Daniel, I fear my lord the king, who hath appointed your meat and your drink: for why should he see your faces worse liking than the children which are of your sort? then shall ye make me endanger my head to the king.

The prince of the eunuchs had good reason to fear the king, for it was common for a court officer to be executed immediately at the displeasure of a dictator (Daniel 6:24). To refuse to consume the food and drink which the king himself provided would be a grave insult to the king himself and to the deity to which the food was likely offered. It was probably unlikely that the king would have had continual communication during the young men's three-year education in the schools of Babylon. The prince of the eunuchs is likely thinking ahead to the end of the three-year period when the young men stand before the king (1:18), and their presumed emaciated appearance would be blamed on himself and would necessitate capital punishment.

[11] Then said Daniel to Melzar, whom the prince of the eunuchs had set over Daniel, Hananiah, Mishael, and Azariah,

Who is Melzar? Melzar is a name of Persian derivation and means "officer, or guardian of the court" in Babylon. Melzar is called the prince of the eunuchs in 1:10 and is a lower ranking and subservient official to Ashpenaz who is called the master of the eunuchs in 1:3. The identification of the young men with their Hebrew names persists even though they have received their Babylonian names. This likely highlights their attempts to resist the pagan influences which contradicted their adherence to the Scriptures.

[12] Prove thy servants, I beseech thee, ten days; and let them give us pulse to eat, and water to drink.

Choosing a non-confrontational approach, Daniel proposes a nonbinding trial to Melzar. Instead of eating the food from the king's table he suggests eating vegetables and herbs, the kind of food which could be eaten in a sort of half-fast, and drinking water instead of wine. Some have likened this diet to a pre-fall diet in the Garden of Eden before meat and possible wine were introduced into the human diet (Genesis 1:29). This so called "Daniel diet" is trying, to say the least! I fully committed to a similar diet consisting of vegetables and water for 10 days, and needless to say I felt frail and fragile and could understand how Melzar would surmise that their outward appearance would be emaciated after an extended pledge to this diet.

[13] Then let our countenances be looked upon before thee, and the countenance of the children that eat of the portion of the king's meat: and as thou seest, deal with thy servants.

Daniel continues to petition the prince of the eunuchs that at the end of the trial their outward appearance be compared to those young men taken captive from other regions in the Fertile Crescent who are dedicated to eating the unclean food at the kings table.

[14] So he consented to them in this matter, and proved them ten days.

Melzar authorized the trial for a period of ten days, likely under the radar of Ashpenaz. The notion of a period of trial being 10 days in duration extends all the way to the book of Revelation (Revelation 2:10).

[15] And at the end of ten days their countenances appeared fairer and fatter in flesh than all the children which did eat the portion of the king's meat.

The undergirding theme of the chapter is that even though the children of Israel are in exile and the Temple is destroyed, the hand of God is with those who are wise. After the ten day trial an idiom is used to express the health of the young men by calling them "fairer and fatter in flesh." This expression pictures a healthy person as solid and plump, the opposite of those who are under siege which are described as "pining away and sticken through for want" (Lamentations 4:9).

[16] Thus Melzar took away the portion of their meat, and the wine that they should drink; and gave them pulse.

After the ten-day examination, the young men's petition to adhere to a kosher diet was likely officially recognized. The remainder of the chapter covers the remaining two years and 11 months in which the young men were enrolled in the learning and tongue of the Chaldeans.

[17] As for these four children, God gave them knowledge and skill in all learning and wisdom: and Daniel had understanding in all visions and dreams.

The hallmark of these young men after their three-year education was their God given ability in knowledge and wisdom. This wisdom came from the same God who gave Jerusalem into the hand of Nebuchadnezzar. Wisdom was highly prized in the courts of Babylon as it was believed to be derived from Marduk or Bel, the god of wisdom. Three different Hebrew words are used synonymously to describe their moral, educational, and religious superiority. Daniel alone though is singled out for his ability to decipher visions. This ability was highly prized in the Ancient Near East and considered a primary source of understanding the will of the gods and even exceeded the ability of being wise. Of course, this insight into the gifts of Daniel prepares the reader for the following chapter and the rest of the book.

[18] Now at the end of the days that the king had said he should bring them in, then the prince of the eunuchs brought them in before Nebuchadnezzar.

Many archeological tablets relating to the lunisolar (indicates both the moon phase and the time of the solar year) calendar of the Babylonians have been found and are on display at the British Museum. One such tablet relates a series of principal events throughout the calendar years of 605-594 BC. Of course, this is of great significance because the entry for the 7th year of the reign of Nebuchadnezzar is locked into the year 598 BC. Nevertheless, the high point of the young men's three years of training has finally arrived as Melzar presents them to the king for their oral and physical examinations.

[19] And the king communed with them; and among them all was found none like Daniel, Hananiah, Mishael, and Azariah: therefore stood they before the king.

Once again, the author introduces the young men via their Hebrew names in order to identify them with the people of God rather than identifying them by their Babylonian theophoric names. As to the reasoning of the order of the names it is understandable why the name Daniel would be first, but some have surmised that Azariah, whose name means "YHWH helps" is rendered last in the list to remind the reader that without YHWH's help none of them would have succeeded in overcoming the things of the world.

[20] And in all matters of wisdom and understanding, that the king inquired of them, he found them ten times better than all the magicians and astrologers that were in all his realm.

As to what actually consisted of the content of their three-year education we are unaware. Nevertheless, a hyperbolic expression meaning "infinitely better" is used to convey the thought that these young men increased more than all that we were with them in Babylon because the God of Israel gave them the skill set needed to overcome such terrific odds. These young men, diligent in their business, stood before kings (Proverbs 22:29). From a literary point of view the number ten appears again, possibly to balance its earlier mention in the narrative.

[21] And Daniel continued even unto the first year of king Cyrus.

Daniel, now a court prophet for King Nebuchadnezzar, would continue in this position of influence in the royal palace throughout the duration of the remaining Neo-Babylonian Empire. Daniel would continue to minister both on and off the political radar through the remaining reigns of Nebuchadnezzar's son Evil Merodach's two year reign (562-560 BC), Neriglissar's four year reign (560-566 BC), Labashi Marduk's three month reign (556 BC), Nabonidus's 17 year reign (556-539 BC), and finally under the reign of the de-facto king Belshazzar's 14 year reign (553-539) as well as ministering in the reign of Cyrus and thereby witnessing the return of the remnant of Judah at the end of the 70 year captivity prophesied by Jeremiah (Jeremiah 25:11). The text makes a point to mention that Daniel stayed in the palace until the first year of Cyrus (this is King Cyrus 2 or Cyrus the Great, the founder of the Medo-Persian Empire). Josephus (Ant. 10.11.7) states that after the first year of Cyrus, Daniel, being around 90 years old moved out of the palace and settled eastward in the city of Susa to close his career. Whatever the case may be, we know that Daniel continued to minister in some capacity because in the third year of the reign of Cyrus (Daniel 10:1) he has a vision of the glory of God by the side of the Tigris/Hiddekel river.

Daniel 2

[1] And in the second year of the reign of Nebuchadnezzar dreamed dreams, wherewith his spirit was troubled, and his sleep brake from him.

The second chapter opens up with a chronological peg that pinpoints the events in this chapter to 603 BC. Nebuchadnezzar, who primarily played a supporting role in the first chapter, now comes to the forefront as the lead character along with Daniel. These events would have happened some three years or so after the first wave of captivity (1:1), and on the heels of the young Hebrew's men education in the learning and tongue of the Chaldeans and their subsequent promotion by Nebuchadnezzar (1:21). Yet, an ancient Greek manuscript (MS 967) dates the events in chapter two to the twelfth, not the second, year. A slip of the ink pen by the scribe in transmission is not uncommon. When the Dead Sea scrolls were discovered and then translated they were compared to the Aleppo Codex, the oldest known complete Hebrew Bible at the time which dated to 1000 AD. When the Aleppo Codex was compared to the Dead Sea scrolls (some 1000+ years older) they were over 95% in agreement. The only major variations were spelling discrepancies and numerical variants. Nevertheless, the majority of our ancient texts record two years. This opening verse does not pose a problem if we take into account two factors. First, we must remember that the education of these young men took place in the ascension year of Nebuchadnezzar, which we could think of as year zero of his reign and took place before the Babylonian New Year holiday *Akitu*, when Nebuchadnezzar would have been coroneted and installed as king and king alone. Therefore, the second year of Nebuchadnezzar would be the third year of the young men's training. Secondly, another possibility is to recall how the ANE reckoned time. An event that occurred whether part or parcel within an hour, day, month or year would be considered to be a full hour, day, month or year. An example of this would be the Lord Jesus being in the heart of the earth three days and three nights (Matthew 12:40) when the duration was Friday starting around 3:00 PM until sometime early Sunday AM. Another worthy mention is Josephus, who states that the second year of Nebuchadnezzar should be interpreted as two years after Babylon's defeat of Egypt (*Antiquities* 10.10.3). The author continues to draw parallels between Daniel and Joseph; the Hebrew prophets in captivity, yet rising through the ranks of a Gentile power after two years (Genesis 41:1) by the unseen hand of God to save the life of multitudes and grow in influence. Just as Nebuchadnezzar's spirit was troubled after the dream, so Pharaoh's spirit was troubled after his dream (Genesis 41:8).

[2] Then the king commanded to call the magicians, and the astrologers, and the sorcerers, and the Chaldeans, for to shew the king his dreams. So they came and stood before the king.

Just as Nebuchadnezzar summons his royal officials to administer to him in a time of distress, so the Pharaoh from the Joseph account does the same (Genesis 41:8). The author of Daniel likely had the Torah memorized and under the guidance of the Holy Spirit is crafting the second chapter of Daniel against the familiar backdrop of the Joseph account. Some have suggested that the above-mentioned guilds are distinct classes of magi. Nevertheless, the term magicians or *chartummim*, is an Egyptian loan word which means a sacred scribe or someone skilled in writing hieroglyphics. If indeed these are Egyptian magicians in the court of Nebuchadnezzar it would fit nicely with Nebuchadnezzar recently defeating Egypt and, like in Israel, exporting international men of distinction for his aid to the royal court in Babylon.

[3] And the king said unto them, I have dreamed a dream, and my spirit was troubled to know the dream.

Once the national and imported international masters of "knowledge" were summoned to the royal court the king informs them that they must interpret or give the understanding of the dream he had the night before.

[4] Then spake the Chaldeans to the king in Syriack, O king, live forever: tell thy servants the dream, and we will shew the interpretation.

The expression "o king, live forever" was a common term of etiquette in the ANE. Bathsheba addressed King David in this manner (1 Kings 1:31), as did Nehemiah to Artaxerxes 1 (Nehemiah 2:3). The humor in this address is that it had just been revealed to the king that indeed he would not live forever and neither would his empire! Here begins the unique literary device of transferring the language of the text from Hebrew to Aramaic. The Aramaic portion of Daniel continues uninterrupted until 7:28. There are other instances, but much shorter in length, wherein the author will change languages in stride. In the book of Jeremiah there are only two verses that were written in Aramaic (10:11-12), the international trade language in the Fertile Crescent since at least the 8th century. It is likely that one of the motives of Jeremiah in transferring from Hebrew to Aramaic was so that the message conveyed in 10:11-12 would be memorized and thus spread along the major trade routes; that there is one God, and that he is the God of Genesis. Along the same lines, the author likely intended to reach a larger demographic by composing this longest section of the Bible written in Aramaic, primarily because this portion of Daniel deals largely with Gentile affairs. By the time the Jews returned to Israel after the decree of Cyrus the people were so entrenched in Aramaic that an interpreter was needed to translate the Bible into the common tongue (Nehemiah 8:8).

[5] The king answered and said to the Chaldeans, The thing is gone from me: if ye will not make known unto me the dream, with the interpretation thereof, ye shall be cut in pieces, and your houses shall be made a dunghill.

Before dangling a carrot before them the king threatens them with utter destruction. This is analogous to ANE treaties of blessings and curses. Literally cutting someone into pieces was a common form of execution in the ANE. It was also known to the ancient Hebrews, as Samuel cut Agag the Amalekite king into pieces (1 Sam. 15:33). According to Babylonian and Persian customs the house in which the condemned lived was sometimes destroyed and left vacant as a visual reminder of a perpetual curse on that household. A similar custom was also known among the Hebrews, who destroyed the temporary abode of Achan and raised over his house a great heap of stones as a monument to the abhorrence of his crime.

[6] But if ye shew the dream, and the interpretation thereof, ye shall receive of me gifts and rewards and great honour: therefore shew me the dream, and the interpretation thereof.

After the threat of annihilation, the king now dangles the carrot of blessings before the wise men. Like the Pharaoh of the Joseph's account the custom of bestowing gifts on the correct interpreter of the dream by the king is here given (Genesis 41:42-43).

[7] They answered again and said, Let the king tell his servants the dream, and we will shew the interpretation of it.

Here we have the beginning of the second round of dialogue between the king and the wise men. The "wise men," especially if some were imported from Egypt, would have been accustomed to the king relaying the dream to them first and then permitting them time to divine the interpretation. Yet, Nebuchadnezzar, likely sensing their foolishness, aims to test their wit by requiring them to perceive both the dream itself and the correct interpretation thereof.

[8] The king answered and said, I know of certainty that ye would gain the time, because ye see the thing is gone from me.

Nebuchadnezzar surmises that the wise men are trying to placate him and buy time to escape or impede their judgment. What does the phrase "the thing is gone from me" mean? Did Nebuchadnezzar forget the dream? Some have suggested that the translation of the statement be instead rendered "the matter is decided by me" or as the Strong's Concordance suggests "the word has gone out from me." it would also be peculiar for the God of Israel to communicate a dream of such great magnitude to someone only to have them forget the entire dream in the morning.

[9] But if ye will not make known unto me the dream, there is but one decree for you: for ye have prepared lying and corrupt words to speak before me, till the time be changed: therefore tell me the dream, and I shall know that ye can shew me the interpretation thereof.

In other words, Nebuchadnezzar certainly memorized the dream and understands that these charlatans are oblivious to the content of the dream but have concocted lying words as a false interpretation to progress their motive. A basis for the king's suspicion may be his belief that these wise men are part and parcel of an internal attempt to overthrow his reign, so, "the time or situation is changed." Kings of the ANE were not hesitant to execute any person or class who they deemed a political threat. King Saul via Doeg executed 85 persons that wore a linen ephod because of their assisting his political adversary, King David (1 Samuel 22:13-19).

[10] The Chaldeans answered before the king, and said, There is not a man upon the earth that can shew the king's matter: therefore there is no king, lord, nor ruler, that asked such things at any magician, or astrologer, or Chaldean.

As we begin the third round of discourse between the king and his court, these "wise men" who are being asked the impossible, unwittingly provide the main point of the chapter; "that it is not in man, God shall give an answer of peace" to the king (Genesis 41:16).

[11] And it is a rare thing that the king requireth, and there is none other that can shew it before the king, except the gods, whose dwelling is not with flesh.

These wise men were taken aback by the king not abiding by the status quo of the ANE and first telling his dream to the court and then letting them spin the proper interpretation. By not abiding by the status quo these men are pressed to confess their incapacity to intercede with the God of Heaven that reveals secrets. The dialogue between the king and his advisors in the royal court is now over.

[12] For this cause the king was angry and very furious, and commanded to destroy all the wise men of Babylon.

After discerning the facts that these enchanting guilds were a charade, the despot becomes angry and furious, a motif to describe his wrath which is also found later in the book (3:13, 19). He immediately makes a decree to execute anyone enrolled in these various guilds connected to the royal court in Babylon, not necessarily those enchanters within the province or located in the entire empire which traversed the entire Fertile Crescent into the Nile Delta. It appears Nebuchadnezzar was on to their possible plot to remove the king from the throne, but certainly he was exhausted at their charades of professing to have the ability as diviners.

[13] And the decree went forth that the wise men should be slain; and they sought Daniel and his fellows to be slain.

Unlike the rulers under the following Media-Persian dynasty who were unable to reverse a decree that had been proclaimed, Nebuchadnezzar the dictator had the ability to pass legislation without any obstacles or having the stigma of shame attached to him if he so changed his mind. Daniel and his fellows were previously willingly or unwillingly absorbed into one of the previous mentioned guilds (likely upon their graduation) and are therefore rounded up to be hastily executed even though they were not present at the meeting between the king and his royal advisors. The preceding foreboding events pave the way for the entrance of Daniel onto the scene to declare and interpret the dream and prove the LORD makes diviners mad, turns wise men backward, makes their knowledge foolishness, and confirms the word of his servant (Isaiah 44:25-26). In other words, to put on display the power of YHWH and the impotence of the Babylonian chief deity Marduk, a supposed dispenser of wisdom.

[14] Then Daniel answered with counsel and wisdom to Arioch the captain of the king's guard, which was gone forth to slay the wise men of Babylon:

At this point in the narrative the scenes shift towards Daniel and his friends, which gives the reader a sense of anticipation that they can indeed put a stop to the royal decree. After the decree went forth Daniel sought out Arioch, the first mention of him in the book. Arioch was the captain of the royal guard, that is to say, the chief of the executioners, and would have likely been an eyewitness to the events that just transpired in the throne room. Arioch is a name that may be familiar to careful Bible readers, as this was the name of a Gentile king from the east who invaded the Holy Land during the time of Abraham (Genesis 14:1). The name Arioch means something like "lion-like" according to Strong's Concordance, but some have suggested that the Babylonian name Eri-Aku means "servant of the moon god." The name Nebuzaradan (meaning "Nebo has given seed") who carried the same title, may also be familiar to careful Bible readers as he too served as the chief executioner of Nebuchadnezzar and was the man who carried out the order to destroy the Temple in Jerusalem with fire and carried the captives into Babylon (2 Kings 25:8-9, Jeremiah 39:9). Daniel followed the proper royal protocol to inquire of the king's decision from Arioch since at this point Daniel did not have instant access to the throne, and Arioch, who was entrusted with carrying out the mass execution, had not yet begun to carry out his orders.

[15] He answered and said to Arioch the king's captain, Why is the decree so hasty from the king? Then Arioch made the thing known to Daniel.

Daniel, seemingly perplexed by the impulsiveness of the harsh and hasty decree, inquires as to what was the cause and effect of the decree. Note that the title for Arioch has changed from the previous verse; this latter designation would be considered more general than the previous.

[16] Then Daniel went in, and desired of the king that he would give him time, and that he would shew the king the interpretation.

Daniel, whom Esther later parallels (at least here), risks life and limb by petitioning the king without invitation for the salvation of his people and the pagan wise men. Proverbs exhorts the reader not to put forth yourself in the presence of the king (Proverbs 25:6). Later in 2:24 the author reveals the proper etiquette for obtaining an audience with the king, included a middle man to arrange a meeting with the king. Once in the unannounced presence of the king Daniel did not beseech him for an unlimited amount of time but for a very near future prearranged appointment between the two concerning the matter which apparently included a brief delay in the executions. It is likely that Nebuchadnezzar remembered from the earlier oral examinations that "Daniel had understanding in all visions and dreams" (1:17).

[17] Then Daniel went to his house, and made the thing known to Hananiah, Mishael, and Azariah, his companions:

The scene now shifts from the royal court to the dormitories of the young men being educated in the learning and tongue of the Babylonians. Once again, the author continues to recognize these young men by their Hebrew names and thus not necessarily identify them with the Babylonian world system, "the mother of harlots and of the abominations of the earth" (Revelation 17:5).

[18] That they would desire mercies of the God of heaven concerning this secret; that Daniel and his fellows should not perish with the rest of the wise men of Babylon.

Up to this point in the book the God of Israel has only been identified as God (Elohim) and Lord (Adonai). In fact, in the entire book of Daniel the only section where the author uses the tetragrammaton (Greek for "four letters"), i.e., the name YHWH, is in chapter 9 where it is used six times (9:2,4,10,13,14,20) in Daniel's great prayer of national repentance and his vision of the seventy sevens. By connecting a place to the name God (Elohim), Daniel is recognizing Elohim as the invisible most High God who ascends above the heights of the clouds and is far above all visible idols made by the hands of man who dwell on earth. The Septuagint translation heightens the situation by adding that Daniel "proclaimed a fast and supplication."

[19] Then was the secret revealed unto Daniel in a night vision. Then Daniel blessed the God of heaven.

After prayer (and supplication if we include the LXX addition) the God of heaven made known to Daniel the dream and the interpretation during the night. Oftentimes God reveals mysteries to his chosen servants at this watch (Genesis 15:12, 28:11, Acts 18:9).

[20] Daniel answered and said, Blessed be the name of God forever and ever: for wisdom and might are his:

The use of the word *baruch* or blessed was and still is a traditional custom at the beginning of a Hebrew prayer to God. A modern-day example would be the prayers for lighting the candles, drinking the wine, and breaking the bread at a Shabbat dinner, all of which begin with (*baruch*); first blessing God. Once again Daniel dispels the notion that the center of all wisdom came from Babylon's chief deity Marduk, the god of wisdom.

[21] And he changeth the times and the seasons: he removeth kings, and setteth up kings: he giveth wisdom unto the wise, and knowledge to them that know understanding:

In his exaltation of the God of heaven, Daniel ascribes him alone as being the force behind all geopolitical events (Job 12:23). He alone oversees and administers the set time and durations of world empires. A similar concept of God being the distributer and confiscator of all things is also found in the prayers of Hannah (1 Samuel 2.1-10), and Mary (Luke 1:46-55).

[22] He revealeth the deep and secret things: he knoweth what is in the darkness, and the light dwelleth with him.

Perhaps Daniel is thinking of the words of Job (Job 12:22). Nevertheless, the notion that the God of heaven and not the astronomical cults of Babylon accurately perceived future events would have been a full-frontal assault on the fabric of Babylonian thought and practice. By placing the contrasting concepts of darkness and light side by side Daniel is stating that the God of heaven is not only the creator of both (Isaiah 45:7), but also that the omniscient God of heaven knows all things. In Scripture darkness is often a metaphor for the mysterious (1 Corinthians 4:5) and light a metaphor for wisdom (Psalm 119:105).

[23] I thank thee, and praise thee, O thou God of my fathers, who hast given me wisdom and might, and hast made known unto me now what we desired of thee: for thou hast now made known unto us the king's matter.

At the beginning of the petition Daniel refers to God in the third person but now switches to the second person. The only other occasion the term "God of my fathers" is used in the Scriptures is in Paul's defense before Felix the governor (Acts 24:14). The term is loaded with theological, cultural, and historical meaning reaching all the way back to the Patriarchs and even Adam. Daniel is identifying himself with the invisible God who dwells between the Cherubim and created the heaven and earth. Daniel continues the concept from chapter one that the God of Israel is the giver of all things (1:2, 1:17). At the end of the thanksgiving Daniel acknowledges that the petition came from his small prayer group by switching from the first-person singular to the first-person plural (we); two or three were gathered together in His name. So, ends the declaration of blessing.

[24] Therefore Daniel went in unto Arioch, whom the king had ordained to destroy the wise men of Babylon: he went and said thus unto him; Destroy not the wise men of Babylon: bring me in before the king, and I will shew unto the king the interpretation.

Immediately after the small prayer meeting ended, Daniel, following the court room etiquette, sought ought Arioch the chief executioner. Daniel's petition was an instant and direct meeting with the king which had been previously authorized by Daniel's previous unauthorized meeting with the king.

[25] Then Arioch brought in Daniel before the king in haste and said thus unto him, I have found a man of the captives of Judah, that will make known unto the king the interpretation.

Expediting Daniel to the throne room, Arioch links himself to the fate of Daniel by taking recognition for discovering the dreamer who will hopefully appease the wrath of the king, yet distancing himself somewhat by downgrading Daniel as a captive. The parallels between Joseph and Daniel continue as the chief butler intermediated to also present the young Hebrew to the king (Genesis 41:12-14). Recall that this is the year 603 BC and only one wave of captivity of Judah has occurred thus far.

[26] The king answered and said to Daniel, whose name was Belteshazzar, Art thou able to make known unto me the dream which I have seen, and the interpretation thereof?

Since Daniel is now in the royal court the author reminds the reader that his Babylonian name is now employed. The same grammatical structure is used to open the dialogue between the king and Daniel as was used between the king and the wise men of Babylon (the king answered and said) in order to give the chapter unity and possibly as a mnemonic (2:5,8).

[27] Daniel answered in the presence of the king, and said, The secret which the king hath demanded cannot the wise men, the astrologers, the magicians, the soothsayers, shew unto the king;

Daniel opens his response to the king with an authoritative yet negative statement. With command he lumps the different guilds of magi together as being incapable of declaring the mystery of the dream and interpretation. He is also possibly affiliating himself with the overarching group of "wise men" to soon prove that the skill to declare the dream and the interpretation did not come from himself but from the God of heaven.

[28] But there is a God in heaven that revealeth secrets, and maketh known to the king Nebuchadnezzar what shall be in the latter days. Thy dream, and the visions of thy head upon thy bed, are these;

Daniel immediately agrees with the "wise men" of Babylon that the secret can only be revealed by those "whose dwelling is not with flesh" (Daniel 2:11). Our first clue as to the content of the dream reveals to the king and the reader that the dream and the interpretation are eschatological in nature. Daniel, like Joseph, begins his discourse with the king by acknowledging the God of the fathers (Genesis 41:16).

[29] As for thee, O king, thy thoughts came into thy mind upon thy bed, what should come to pass hereafter: and he that revealeth secrets maketh known to thee what shall come to pass.

Daniel, like Joseph, confirms that a correct interpretation of a dream only belongs to God (Genesis 40:8). The phrases "as for thee" and in the next verse "as for me" function as a bridge to link the common knowledge of the end times dream found between Daniel and the king.

[30] But as for me, this secret is not revealed to me for any wisdom that I have more than any living, but for their sakes that shall make known the interpretation to the king, and that thou mightest know the thoughts of thy heart.

While concluding his preface before he begins to declare the content and interpretation of the dream, Daniel informs us that the dream came as an answer to the king's desire to know the course and end of world powers in the future.

[31] Thou, O king, sawest, and behold a great image. This great image, whose brightness was excellent, stood before thee; and the form thereof was terrible.

The first image the king was given in his dream was of a singular massive and dreadful statue or idol, emphasizing its monolithic nature.

[32] This image's head was of fine gold, his breast and his arms of silver, his belly and his thighs of brass, [33] His legs of iron, his feet part of iron and part of clay.

The image's worth which is being compared to precious metals and alloys decreases in a fivefold manner from top to bottom while simultaneously the image's metals or alloys, that is to say its military strength, increases from top to bottom.

[34] Thou sawest till that a stone was cut out without hands, which smote the image upon his feet that were of iron and clay, and brake them to pieces.

The emphasis given in this passage is that the stone (headstone?) is not a product or creation from the hand of man, but is supernatural in its origin, nature and cataclysmic mission. After the phrase "cut out without hands" the LXX adds the phrase "from a mountain" which correlates with vs. 45 and ties the stones source to a mountain. Throughout the Scriptures the LORD God's abode or presence is on a mountain (Exodus 3:1, 20:18, 1 Kings 19:8-18, Matthew 17:1-8, etc.).

[35] Then was the iron, the clay, the brass, the silver, and the gold, broken to pieces together, and became like the chaff of the summer threshingfloors; and the wind carried them away, that no place was found for them: and the stone that smote the image became a great mountain, and filled the whole earth.

Since the image is monolithic in nature each metal or alloy is melded or interconnected with the other and is destroyed upon the stones impact, hence the reverse order. The manner in which the author describes the destruction and subsequent scattering of the image is loaded with an agricultural and textual history. The two staples of the ancient Israelite economy were the farmer and shepherd. In fact, these are the two oldest recorded professions in the text (Genesis 4:2). After the reaper thrust in his sickle and gathered the wheat or barley from the field (barley harvest always precedes the wheat harvest and often occurred in ancient Israel in April/May while the wheat harvest came in May/June) it was transported to a nearby threshing floor where the process of separating the grain from the chaff began. Once the wheat or barley was ground under the threshing sled by a beast of burden the community would carefully separate the intertwined good from the bad by tossing both in the air, where the winds would take the light and worthless chaff away, and only the precious wheat or barley would remain. Oftentimes in the Scriptures God's judgment is associated with the worthless chaff driven away (Job 21:8, Psalm 1:4, 35:5, Isaiah 17:3, Matthew 3:12, etc.). The stone, being divine in its source and mission, not only destroys and replaces the image and its function but establishes a kingdom of its own.

[36] This is the dream; and we will tell the interpretation thereof before the king.

So, ends the content of the dream revealed by the God of heaven to Daniel and the commencement of the interpretation to the king.

[37] Thou, O king, art a king of kings: for the God of heaven hath given thee a kingdom, power, and strength, and glory.

The term" king of kings" was a common expression of respect directed towards ANE kings (Ezra 7:12, Ezekiel 26:70). The title was later used by early Christians in expressing their reverence to their king, the Lord Jesus (1 Timothy 6:15, Revelation 17:4, 19: 16). Daniel informs the king that the source of his authority and dominion comes from an otherwise unknown god to the king; the God of heaven.

[38] And wheresoever the children of men dwell, the beasts of the field and the fowls of the heaven hath he given into thine hand, and hath made thee ruler over them all. Thou art this head of gold.

Daniel continues to inform the king that the God of heaven has bestowed all of creation under the authority of the king, the LXX adds the phrase "and the fish of the sea" in order to fill out his rule over all creation. Of course, this dominion should reminder the reader of the same authority and dominion that the God of heaven bestowed upon Adam (Genesis 1:26). This would now even include the city of Jerusalem. Nebuchadnezzar would be the first of four empires to dominate the City of the Great King. The king was likely ignorant of the fact that this declaration was indeed the fulfillment of a prophecy of the prophet Jeremiah that Daniel was likely familiar with (Jeremiah 27:6-7). Nevertheless, the captive reader finally is informed that King Nebuchadnezzar and the remaining gentile Neo-Babylonian Empire (605-539 BC) are indeed represented in the image as the head of gold.

[39] And after thee shall arise another kingdom inferior to thee, and another third kingdom of brass, which shall bear rule over all the earth.

The second kingdom is immediately represented by Daniel as being inferior to the Babylonian Empire in worth, that is to say in their form of government, but as previously mentioned is stronger in their military might. The second kingdom is separated from the head into two distinct members, which history has shown to be the empire of the Medes and Persians (539-331 BC). The third kingdom is characterized as inferior in worth to the first and second kingdoms but stronger in force. History has shown this to be the Greek Empire (331-146 BC).

[40] And the fourth kingdom shall be strong as iron: forasmuch as iron breaketh in pieces and subdueth all things: and as iron that breaketh all these, shall it break in pieces and bruise.

The fourth kingdom is without delay characterized as destructive in its nature, being strong and fierce in its military might. Yet the form of their government being symbolized as iron is a far cry from the worth of the original gold-standard Babylonian Empire. History has shown this last empire to be the Roman Empire (146 BC-395 AD). Like the Medio-Persian empire which consisted of two entities, this portion of the image is later described as standing on two legs (395-1453 AD). After the death of the Emperor Theodosius in 395 AD the Roman Empire was split into two, a western empire ruled from Rome and an eastern empire ruled from Constantinople. The western empire soon dissolved while the eastern empire maintained itself for another 1000 years or so.

[41] And whereas thou sawest the feet and toes, part of potters' clay, and part of iron, the kingdom shall be divided; but there shall be in it of the strength of the iron, forasmuch as thou sawest the iron mixed with miry clay.

An outgrowth of the fourth and final kingdom is described as politically and militarily weaker than all others and is divided into ten toes or kings which are here mentioned for the first time. The thread of ten kings ruling under the umbrella of Gentile rule is a prominent theme in New Testament eschatology (Revelation 13:1, 17:12).

[42] And as the toes of the feet were part of iron, and part of clay, so the kingdom shall be partly strong, and partly broken.

In the mindset of the ANE clay would have symbolized fragility and great weakness (Job 4:19, 13:12, Psalm 2:9, etc.). Therefore, the author strives to make the point that even though there is a residue of the old Roman Empire in the final stages of the "time of the Gentiles" (Luke 21:24) the final empire divided into ten kings is feeble compared to the kingdom out of which it grew.

[43] And whereas thou sawest iron mixed with miry clay, they shall mingle themselves with the seed of men: but they shall not cleave one to another, even as iron is not mixed with clay.

The final stage of Gentile world power before the stone smites it is characterized by its lack of cohesion as it unsuccessfully attempts to unite the nations of the world. The final form of Gentile government is directly opposed to the first form of Gentile government which was considered monolithic in rule and pristine in its gold standard form of government.

[44] And in the days of these kings shall the God of heaven set up a kingdom, which shall never be destroyed: and the kingdom shall not be left to other people, but it shall break in pieces and consume all these kingdoms, and it shall stand for ever.

During the diluted or weakened form of the Roman government which is characterized by the rule of ten toes or kings (Revelation 13:1), the God of heaven will send the stone to annihilate the time of Gentile rule over Jerusalem and the earth and to establish his mountain or theocratic form of government on earth (Jerusalem) permanently.

[45] Forasmuch as thou sawest that the stone was cut out of the mountain without hands, and that it brake in pieces the iron, the brass, the clay, the silver, and the gold; the great God hath made known to the king what shall come to pass hereafter: and the dream is certain, and the interpretation thereof sure.

As Daniel finishes the interpretation he summarizes the dream and reminds the king which deity, albeit likely unknown to Nebuchadnezzar at this time, revealed the dream to him. Daniel also reminds the king that the dream from the great God is (*yatstsiyb*) established or valid and the interpretation is (*'aman*) trustworthy. Daniel begins and ends his discourse before the king by honoring the God of his fathers.

[46] Then the king Nebuchadnezzar fell upon his face, and worshipped Daniel, and commanded that they should offer an oblation and sweet odours unto him.

When Daniel ceased speaking the king arose from his throne and covered his face in the earth to publicly display his veneration to the God of heaven and the prophet Daniel even though the dream contains the termination of his government. The king then commands his officers to bestow grain (*minchah*) and incense upon Daniel so that he may present them as an offering to his God.

[47] The king answered unto Daniel, and said, Of a truth it is, that your God is a God of gods, and a Lord of kings, and a revealer of secrets, seeing thou couldest reveal this secret.

The final words of Nebuchadnezzar in this royal throne room scene are words of praise to Daniel's God as he recognizes Him to be the supreme deity in the heavens above (God of gods) and over the kings of the earth (Lord of kings).

[48] Then the king made Daniel a great man, and gave him many great gifts, and made him ruler over the whole province of Babylon, and chief of the governors over all the wise men of Babylon.

Continuing the parallels between Daniel and Joseph, the author gives special attention to the material gifts bestowed upon the young Hebrew prophet by the Gentile king upon the interpretation of the dream (Genesis 41:40-44). Such physical gifts would have likely made Daniel a rich man, but the designation of his new high position within the social fabric of Babylonia would now give him tremendous sway in the inner workings of the kingdom. Daniel's first newly appointed position consisted of having dominion over the imperial province and the capital city of the empire. His second position made him prefect over all the guilds of the Babylonian magi which likely included certain religious freedoms for himself and his friends.

[49] Then Daniel requested of the king, and he set Shadrach, Meshach, and Abed-nego, over the affairs of the province of Babylon: but Daniel sat in the gate of the king.

Seizing the moment, Daniel possibly reminded the king that he was not alone in the process of determining the dream and the interpretation and therefore petitioned the king that honor should be bestowed upon those who assisted him, namely his three Hebrew friends. Nebuchadnezzar grants Daniel's request and promotes the three young men as administrators under the authority of Daniel. Yet the king persists in highlighting the superiority of Daniel as a wise man and gives him public honor by positioning him with one of the highest level of cabinet rank; seated in the gate of the city as the eyes and ears of Nebuchadnezzar (Genesis 19:1, Deuteronomy 16:18, Ruth 4:1).

Daniel 3

[1] Nebuchadnezzar the king made an image of gold, whose height was threescore cubits, and the breadth thereof six cubits: he set it up in the plain of Dura, in the province of Babylon.

On the heels of the revelation that he indeed is the head of gold, Nebuchadnezzar (Nabu, god of Babylon, protect the borders) orders the construction of an image. The text does not make it clear if the image is of the king himself or of the chief deity Marduk. In line with the customs of the ANE it is likely that the image was not constructed of solid gold but consisted of an inexpensive material like mud bricks which was then covered with thin sheets of gold (Jeremiah 10:3-4). Larger than life statues were common in the ANE. I have seen a 42-foot-high statue of Ramses 2 at Memphis in Egypt. If we use the standard cubit (18") the height of the 60-cubit image would have been 90 feet high and 9-foot wide. If we use the royal cubit (21") the height would have been over 100 feet high and 10-foot wide. It is probable that the dimensions were chosen for architectural efficiency but also because the number 60 was sacred to the Babylonian god Anu (heaven). Perhaps these are the same dimensions of the image Nebuchadnezzar saw in the vision of the previous chapter. As for the location of the event, the Babylonian word *Dura* means "dwelling" though some have suggested it means "wall." If Dura means wall it is possible the ceremony could have taken place between the outer and inner walls of the city of Babylon or some have even suggested it could have taken place in the city of Dura situated on the banks of the Tigris River or another site with the same name located on the banks of the Euphrates River. The exact location of the place name still eludes Biblical geographers.

[2] Then Nebuchadnezzar the king sent to gather together the princes, the governors, and the captains, the judges, the treasurers, the counsellers, the sheriffs, and all the rulers of the provinces, to come to the dedication of the image which Nebuchadnezzar the king had set up.

A royal decree was issued throughout the empire requesting the presence of all local and federal state representatives. The ANE custom of the government summoning the political elite for a religious ceremony was quite common as apparently King Solomon did the same (1 Kings 8:1). The exact function or responsibilities of the offices of these seven classes of Babylonian hierarchy is not clear. It is likely that the list is in a descending order. The ANE custom of dedicating an object for religious reasons was also common in the ANE as the ancient Israelites dedicated the altar of the Tabernacle (Numbers 7:10) and King Solomon dedicated the Temple in Jerusalem (1 Kings 8:63).

[3] Then the princes, the governors, and captains, the judges, the treasurers, the counsellers, the sheriffs, and all the rulers of the provinces, were gathered together unto the dedication of the image that Nebuchadnezzar the king had set up; and they stood before the image that Nebuchadnezzar had set up.

After an undisclosed amount of time the hierarchy of the Babylonian government gathered for the theocratic ceremony. The recitation of the list of dignitaries is likely used to heighten the drama of the scene. To emphasize that Nebuchadnezzar himself ordained the ceremony the author repeats that the king set up the image.

[4] Then an herald cried aloud, To you it is commanded, O people, nations, and languages,

At the appointed time, a professional orator from the guild of the heralds began his prescribed public proclamation with force. The terms used for the recipients of the proclamation (people, nations, and languages) is an all-encompassing description of the ethnic, political and linguistic people groups under the rule and reign of Nebuchadnezzar.

[5] That at what time ye hear the sound of the cornet, flute, harp, sackbut, psaltery, dulcimer, and all kinds of musick, ye fall down and worship the golden image that Nebuchadnezzar the king hath set up:

The verse attests to the fondness Babylonian monarchs had towards music. The six specific instruments are from the wind, stringed and percussion (rhythm) families. They had numerous instruments and organized orchestras. Annarus, a Babylonian noble, entertained his guests at a banquet of music – vocal and instrumental – with a choir of 150 women. The proclamation to fall down and worship the image posed a tremendous problem for the Hebrews as it was forbidden to bow down and worship the image made in the likeness of either Nebuchadnezzar or Marduk the Babylonian god (Exodus 20:5).

[6] And whoso falleth not down and worshippeth shall the same hour be cast into the midst of a burning fiery furnace.

This is the first indication in scripture of so short a division of time. *Shaah*, "hour" is a vague expression without a definite time attached to the meaning as we understand by the word hour. It is interesting because it is purported that the Babylonians were the first to make divisions in the 24-hour cycle. The Greeks learned it from them (Herodotus, 2, 109), and the Jews likely learned it from the Babylonians as well. There is no allusion to the unit of an hour before the Babylonian captivity. After the captivity, there is frequent usage of the term (John 11:9). The effect of disobeying the decree to bow down and serve the image would seemingly result in instant death. A decree of the death penalty followed by immediate punishment reminds us of the policy issued in the previous chapter. The construction of mud brick making and producing the necessary heat for baking to construct the furnace and flame was common in the ANE as early as the narrative of the Tower of Babel (Genesis 11:3). Some have suggested that the furnace was located in the image itself.

[7] Therefore at that time, when all the people heard the sound of the cornet, flute, harp, sackbut, psaltery, and all kinds of musick, all the people, the nations, and the languages, fell down and worshipped the golden image that Nebuchadnezzar the king had set up.

The word "therefore" begins to convey the logical outcome of the pressure exercised by the king which was immediate and in total obedience.

[8] Wherefore at that time certain Chaldeans came near, and accused the Jews.

Just at the time (wherefore) the proclamation was made some from the guild of the magi reported to the king an accusation. The Aramaic word for accusation (*qerats*) is a violent word that not only means slander but conveys the idea of verbal cannibalism or the Chaldeans maliciously chewing on the Hebrews. Throughout the whole book it is only in this chapter (3:8, 3:12) that the term Jew is used and in both instances here it is likely used in a derogatory way.

[9] They spake and said to the king Nebuchadnezzar, O king, live for ever.

Before the Chaldeans reprove the Jews, they begin their dialogue with a customary salutation of admiration to the king.

[10] Thou, O king, hast made a decree, that every man that shall hear the sound of the cornet, flute, harp, sackbut, psaltery, and dulcimer, and all kinds of musick, shall fall down and worship the golden image: [11] And whoso falleth not down and worshippeth, that he should be cast into the midst of a burning fiery furnace.

The Chaldeans remind the king of his status as the head of gold and that his policies once implemented cannot be disobeyed.

[12] There are certain Jews whom thou hast set over the affairs of the province of Babylon, Shadrach, Meshach, and Abed-nego; these men, O king, have not regarded thee: they serve not thy gods, nor worship the golden image which thou hast set up.

Unfortunately for the king these were not common Jews who disobeyed the direct order of the king but men whom he had previously established as administrators of the province of Babylon. The refusal of the Hebrews to adopt the pagan customs of the Babylonians and their appointment to the highest offices of the kingdom was apparently a source of intense bitterness and jealousy among their peers, who were likely waiting for the opportunity to burn them. The Chaldeans make it a point to inform the king that the supposed rebellion of the Hebrews in not complying with the decree of the king would have brought public shame to the king who had previously promoted them.

[13] Then Nebuchadnezzar in his rage and fury commanded to bring Shadrach, Meshach, and Abed-nego. Then they brought these men before the king.

After hearing the report from the magi of the defection of his appointed counselors, the countenance of the king is described in two words meaning "to be placed next to each other" which conveys the idea of hysterical rage.

[14] Nebuchadnezzar spake and said unto them, Is it true, O Shadrach, Meshach, and Abed-nego, do not ye serve my gods, nor worship the golden image which I have set up?

Possibly in a tone of disbelief the king questions his recent government appointees if the accusations that they are not subservient to the gods of Babylon are valid. The king is likely not so much concerned with their private beliefs but with their public conduct.

[15] Now if ye be ready that at what time ye hear the sound of the cornet, flute, harp, sackbut, psaltery, and dulcimer, and all kinds of musick, ye fall down and worship the image which I have made; well: but if ye worship not, ye shall be cast the same hour into the midst of a burning fiery furnace; and who is that God that shall deliver you out of my hands?

Surprisingly the king attempts to persuade the Hebrews and offers them a second chance to rethink their insubordination and obey the royal decree. The same God who gave Jerusalem into Nebuchadnezzar's hand (1:2) is now being challenged as to his ability to deliver the Hebrew boys out of Nebuchandnezzar's own hand. The king turns his conflict with the Hebrew boys into a duel with their God.

[16] Shadrach, Meshach, and Abed-nego, answered and said to the king, O Nebuchadnezzar, we are not careful to answer thee in this matter.

The response of the Hebrews to the king is one of respect but is also a challenge to the king that they are not obligated to respond to his confrontation directed at their God. Neither the king's glowing words nor the heat of the visible furnace were enough to persuade them to violate the torah of their God.

[17] If it be so, our God whom we serve is able to deliver us from the burning fiery furnace, and he will deliver us out of thine hand, O king.

The *if or if not* scenario presented to the king by the Hebrews corresponds to the same *if or if not* scenario the king previously employed (3:15). The Hebrews are not questioning the power of God but are uncertain of His will and plan because they do not know if God will perform a miracle on this occasion. They knew miracles were rare (Judges 6:13) and many righteous saints were "tortured, not accepting deliverance" (Hebrews 11:35).

[18] But if not, be it known unto thee, O king, that we will not serve thy gods, nor worship the golden image which thou hast set up.

Jeremiah the prophet exhorted the Jews in captivity to submit to their authorities and even to pray for their Gentile overlords (Jeremiah 29:7). But what is right in God's eyes? To obey the king or God (Acts 4:19)? The Hebrews respectfully but defiantly inform the king that they cannot submit to his royal decree.

[19] Then was Nebuchadnezzar full of fury, and the form of his visage was changed against Shadrach, Meshach, and Abed-nego: therefore he spake, and commanded that they should heat the furnace one seven times more than it was wont to be heated.

There is a progression in the wrath of the king from the beginning of the conversation (3:13). The internal rage of the king boiled over into an outward appearance of frenzy. Even though lowering the temperature of the furnace would have prolonged the agony of the Hebrews the king commands the furnace to be heated as hot as it could be. Some have suggested the temperature could have exceeded 1000 degrees.

[20] And he commanded the most mighty men that were in his army to bind Shadrach, Meshach, and Abed-nego, and to cast them into the burning fiery furnace.

On the cliff face engraving at Khorsabad (modern day N. Iraq) there are representations of strong men, like the "mighty men" mentioned here, who seem to have often or always been in a kings presence. I surmise it can be analogous to the secret service. These men, chosen from the military ranks because of their brawn, took the three boys and cast them into the fiery furnace.

[21] Then these men were bound in their coats, their hosen, and their hats, and their other garments, and were cast into the midst of the burning fiery furnace.

It is difficult to pinpoint the exact meaning of these articles of clothing but good suggestions have been proposed. Coats were likely mantles, and gave the distinctive feature of ANE dress. Hosen were likely inner tunics. Hats were an upper tunic. Garments were likely a cloak worn over all other articles.

[22] Therefore because the king's commandment was urgent, and the furnace exceeding hot, the flame of the fire slew those men that took up Shadrach, Meshach, and Abed-nego.

The mighty men who apprehended the Hebrews were instantly incinerated by the flames which could have exceeded 1000 degrees because of the king's harsh (*chatsaph*) or insolent decree. Because the mighty men "took up" (*necaq*) the Hebrews, which denotes an upward movement, they were likely thrown into the furnace through an opening at the top.

[23] And these three men, Shadrach, Meshach, and Abed-nego, fell down bound into the midst of the burning fiery furnace.

The author likely uses the number three to set up the reader for the appearance of a fourth person in the fire. We are reminded that they were bound in order to heighten the drama of them soon being unbound.

[24] Then Nebuchadnezzar the king was astonished, and rose up in haste, and spake, and said unto his counsellers, Did not we cast three men bound into the midst of the fire? They answered and said unto the king, True, O king.

The amazed and alarmed king arose from his throne at a comfortable distance and inquired of his advisors of what he already knew.

[25] He answered and said, Lo, I see four men loose, walking in the midst of the fire, and they have no hurt; and the form of the fourth is like the Son of God.

The king continues the dialogue with his advisors by being the first to notice the miraculous appearance of the fourth man who unbound the three previously seized men. The fact that these men are unhurt is in contrast with the mighty men who were just slain by the fire. The supernatural deliverance of the Hebrews made a tremendous impact on the nation of Israel as some 400 years later the author of First Maccabees states "Hananiah, Azariah, and Mishael believed and were saved from the flame" (1 Maccabees 2:59) in order to encourage his fellow Israelites to withstand the onslaught from Antiochus Epiphanes. Unfortunately, the King James translation is slightly incorrect in its identification of the fourth person as the Son of God, a term never used in the Hebrew Bible. The correct translation should be "a son of the gods." Most assuredly the Lord Jesus appeared to Moses out of the burning bush (John 8:58, etc.) and others have thought to have seen other appearances of the pre-incarnate Christ in the Tenach. Therefore, there is no theological reason why he could not have appeared to deliver his servants in the flame, yet it is not dogmatic that it indeed was Jesus as later the fourth man is called an angel or messenger. Nevertheless, the fourth man, whoever it may be (the Talmud says it was Gabriel) was sent from the third heaven by God.

[26] Then Nebuchadnezzar came near to the mouth of the burning fiery furnace, and spake, and said, Shadrach, Meshach, and Abed-nego, ye servants of the most high God, come forth, and come hither. Then Shadrach, Meshach, and Abed-nego, came forth of the midst of the fire.

The Hebrews that quenched the violence of fire were greeted at the side door of the furnace by the bedazzled king who now addressed their God as the Most High God. That description of God as being supreme is primarily only used by non-Hebrews and is utilized in the book of Daniel and in the narrative of Abraham and Melchizedek, the narrative of Balaam (Numbers 24:16), and the king of Babylon (Isaiah 14:14) as well as by Asaph in Psalm 78:56 throughout the Tenach.

[27] And the princes, governors, and captains, and the king's counsellers, being gathered together, saw these men, upon whose bodies the fire had no power, nor was an hair of their head singed, neither were their coats changed, nor the smell of fire had passed on them.

The verse begins with an abridged list of the administrators of the king who witnessed the miracle. These dignitaries or witnesses would have represented the eyes and ears of the entire empire. When the God of Israel chooses to deliver he does so completely. As none of the Israelites were slain by the Angel of Death in Egypt, or none lacked for food in the wilderness, and as none were harmed in the crossing of the Reed Sea, so these Hebrews escaped the fire unmolested.

[28] Then Nebuchadnezzar spake, and said, Blessed be the God of Shadrach, Meshach, and Abed-nego, who hath sent his angel, and delivered his servants that trusted in him, and have changed the king's word, and yielded their bodies, that they might not serve nor worship any god, except their own God.

Nebuchadnezzar's praise of God begins with "Blessed be the God" which only appears here in the Hebrew Bible. He continues to esteem the God of the Hebrews for the miracle and praises the Hebrews for not worshiping any god but their own. This may be a clue that the image erected by Nebuchadnezzar was indeed not of himself but of the chief deity Marduk.

[29] Therefore I make a decree, That every people, nation, and language, which speak any thing amiss against the God of Shadrach, Meshach, and Abed-nego, shall be cut in pieces, and their houses shall be made a dunghill: because there is no other God that can deliver after this sort.

Instead of worshiping the golden image those attending the ceremony and those they govern throughout the empire are now commanded with the highest level of proclamation to worship the God of the Hebrews with the form of punishment for disobedience analogous to the chastisement decreed upon the magi in the previous chapter.

[30] Then the king promoted Shadrach, Meshach, and Abed-nego, in the province of Babylon.

Finally, the king quickly caused to prosper or promoted the Hebrews to great public honor by readmitting them to the rank and file of the Babylonian empire. Interestingly the third chapter of Daniel in the Hebrew Bible continues through chapter 4:3 in the English translation.

Daniel 4

[1] Nebuchadnezzar the king, unto all people, nations, and languages, that dwell in all the earth; Peace be multiplied unto you.

As previously mentioned the Hebrew scribes thought it prudent to include the first three verses of chapter four as the last three verses of chapter three. The proclamation sent from the epicenter of Babylonian would reach the entire Babylonian kingdom which encompassed essentially the entire Fertile Crescent (Israel, Edom, Moab, Ammon, Lebanon, Syria, modern day Iraq, part of Iran and Egypt) and also extended into lower Asia Minor (modern day Turkey). The king begins his proclamation with a message of comfort, wishing shalom or completeness or wholeness upon all his subjects and wishing that their prosperity would increase.

[2] I thought it good to shew the signs and wonders that the high God hath wrought toward me.

Nebuchadnezzar proclaims to the end of the earth (his kingdom) the miracle he recently witnessed by the hand of Elohim, the God of the Hebrews, who delivered his three servants from the fiery furnace.

[3] How great are his signs! and how mighty are his wonders! his kingdom is an everlasting kingdom, and his dominion is from generation to generation.

The king finishes his proclamation of praise to the supreme God by revering his power and acknowledging his authority as king of kings and eternal power. The description of God's kingdom and dominion in this manner is only used one another time in the Tenach and that is by King David (Psalm 145:13).

[4] I Nebuchadnezzar was at rest in mine house, and flourishing in my palace:

According to the 5th century BC Greek historian Herodotus, the ancient city of Babylon was 14 miles square on each side, surrounded by a 56-mile-long wall which was 300 feet high and 25 feet thick with eight gates. The secondary wall was 75 feet behind the first wall and constructed some 35 feet deep into the ground. There were reportedly over 250 towers reaching hundreds of feet high. To ensure an even greater defense there was a moat encircling the entire city. The streets of the city were paved with slab stones three-foot square that lead to the famous Hanging Gardens of Babylon and over 50 temples and countless altars to Ishtar. And the jewel of the city was the setting for this chapter, the famous Palace of Nebuchadnezzar which was considered to be the most magnificent building ever built on earth. This is where the king was free from care and was prospering or thriving.

[5] I saw a dream which made me afraid, and the thoughts upon my bed and the visions of my head troubled me.

Before describing the content of the dream, the king depicts his fear. Some commentators date the events in this chapter to 570 BC. If that is the case the events of chapter four are 33 years after the king's initial dream in chapter two and 15 years after the deliverance of the Hebrews from the fiery furnace. Approximately two years before the dream Nebuchadnezzar conquered the city of Tyre (Ezekiel 29:17-18) and Egypt according to the word of the Lord through Jeremiah the prophet (Jeremiah 44:29-30). According to a fragmentary clay tablet, shortly after this dream in 568 BC, Nebuchadnezzar marched to Egypt to quell a revolt (ANET 308).

[6] Therefore made I a decree to bring in all the wise men of Babylon before me, that they might make known unto me the interpretation of the dream.

Continuing the discourse in the first person the king summons the guilds of wise men to throne room to reveal not the dream itself but the interpretation thereof. A number of elements in this narrative remind the reader of the events of chapter two.

[7] Then came in the magicians, the astrologers, the Chaldeans, and the soothsayers: and I told the dream before them; but they did not make known unto me the interpretation thereof.

Parallel to chapter two the "wise men" of Babylon are summoned to interpret the dream but are dismissed in shame for failing to understand the dream at the appointed time. Nebuchadnezzar possibly did not require the magi to tell him the content of the dream in order to soothe his troubled mind.

[8] But at the last Daniel came in before me, whose name was Belteshazzar, according to the name of my god, and in whom is the spirit of the holy gods: and before him I told the dream, saying,

Once the foolishness had ended the prophet of the Most High God entered the throne room. The author is again drawing parallels between Joseph and Daniel as Joseph is also recognized by the Gentile king as possessing "the spirit of God" (Genesis 41:38). Nebuchadnezzar is likely attributing the supernatural gifts of Daniel to his deity Bel by stating that Daniel's name or identity is based in Bel the god of Babylon.

[9] O Belteshazzar, master of the magicians, because I know that the spirit of the holy gods is in thee, and no secret troubleth thee, tell me the visions of my dream that I have seen, and the interpretation thereof.

Possibly Nebuchadnezzar, like Ahab the king, waited until his "yes men" were finished before summoning Daniel, knowing that the interpretation was likely foreboding (1 Kings 22:8). This is the first time Daniel's new title "master of the magicians" appears in the text but is similar to his designation given some 30 years earlier (2:48). Overtime a reputation that nothing was too difficult for Daniel became so prominent that Ezekiel uses Daniel as the epitome of wisdom while taunting the king of Tyre (Ezekiel 28:3).

[10] Thus were the visions of mine head in my bed; I saw, and behold a tree in the midst of the earth, and the height thereof was great.

The symbol of a tree in Scripture can be symbolic of a strong and mighty king (Ezekiel 31) as well as representing the growth of a kingdom (Luke 13:19). The tree can also signify a righteous (Psalm 1:3) or wicked person (Malachi 4:1). The detail that the tree was in the middle of the earth suggests the centrality of the empire in the affairs of the world. Also, the fact that the tree was in the midst reminds the reader of the tree of life "in the midst of the garden" (Genesis 2:9). The ancient Babylonian ziggurat built in the 6th century called Etemenanki (the foundation of heaven and earth) along with other clues suggest the Babylonians believed their city was the center of the earth.

[11] The tree grew, and was strong, and the height thereof reached unto heaven, and the sight thereof to the end of all the earth:

The kingdom (yet to be identified) expanded its borders (grew) and military dominance (was strong) throughout the world, and the magnificence and brilliance of the form of government connected heaven to earth. The reader should be reminded of the attempted construction of the Tower of Babel whose aim was "to reach unto heaven" (Genesis 11:4).

[12] The leaves thereof were fair, and the fruit thereof much, and in it was meat for all: the beasts of the field had shadow under it, and the fowls of the heaven dwelt in the boughs thereof, and all flesh was fed of it.

The kingdom is identified as being seen by the whole world, as being prosperous, and as producing enough food to provide for the needs of all peoples, languages, and nations. The Nebuchadnezzar twin inscriptions of Brisa (ANET 307) carved on two rock faces near the Beqa Valley in Lebanon have been suggested by some in part to read "under its everlasting shadow I have gathered all the peoples in peace." If this is a correct translation it indeed reflects similar language to this verse in the function of Nebuchadnezzar as the provider and sustainer of the world.

[13] I saw in the visions of my head upon my bed, and, behold, a watcher and an holy one came down from heaven;

Suddenly a watcher, even a holy one, appears on the scene from the third heaven. Its designation is a *hendiadys* and describes one heavenly being. The designation as an angel being a watcher only appears in the book of Daniel throughout the Hebrew Bible (Daniel 4:13, 23). Watcher is also a name for angels in later Hebrew writings (Book of Enoch).

[14] He cried aloud, and said thus, Hew down the tree, and cut off his branches, shake off his leaves, and scatter his fruit: let the beasts get away from under it, and the fowls from his branches:

The declaration from the third heaven is the impending destruction of the yet to be named kingdom. The enemies of Jeremiah similarly declared "let us destroy the tree (Jeremiah) with the fruit thereof and let us cut him off" (Jeremiah 11:19).

[15] Nevertheless leave the stump of his roots in the earth, even with a band of iron and brass, in the tender grass of the field; and let it be wet with the dew of heaven, and let his portion be with the beasts in the grass of the earth:

The bigger they are the harder they fall! Though the foreboding oracle calls for the tree to be cut down, yet through scent of water, or over time the stock will again bud, leaving the king with a hope of the tree's restoration. At the end of the oracle against the Pharaoh (Ezekiel 31:18) the author transfers the imagery from tree to human imagery. The author here does the same by stating the tree/person will soon be imprisoned in the field with fetters whose only company is the beasts of the field. There is an ironic turn of events as the tree who once provided shelter for the beasts now only has them to comfort him in his prison.

[16] Let his heart be changed from man's, and let a beast's heart be given unto him; and let seven times pass over him.

The heart when spoken of figuratively was considered to be the inner control center of the ancient Israelites. The word is used over 800 times in the Scriptures. Out of the heart flowed all the issues of life (Proverbs 4:23) and it was the location of character (Luke 6:45). It is the aspect of man wherewith God is most concerned (1 Samuel 16:7). The demeanor, conduct, and appearance of the man will be changed into that of a beast for seven (*shiba*) times (*iddan*). *Iddan* is an Aramaic word which means a time of duration or a year. As a result, the man is sentenced to a seven-year open-air imprisonment. The medieval French Rabbi Rashi suggested that the seven-year sentence imposed on Nebuchadnezzar was in retribution for the Solomonic Temple which he destroyed that took seven years to build (1 Kings 6:1,38).

[17] This matter is by the decree of the watchers, and the demand by the word of the holy ones: to the intent that the living may know that the most High ruleth in the kingdom of men, and giveth it to whomsoever he will, and setteth up over it the basest of men.

The king's sentence is determined and delivered by the angelic court for the purpose that the entire Babylonian Empire and even those beyond its borders may recognize the God of the Hebrews, the Most High God, as the only wise God. This angelic court would be "all them that are about" God in the throne room of heaven (Psalm 89:7). The author is contrasting the glory of the Most High God with the rulers of the earth which are considered the basest or lowliest of men in comparison to God. Every single ruler of the nations of the world from the beginning to this very day has been given that position by the divine intervention of the Most High God (Daniel 4:25).

[18] This dream I king Nebuchadnezzar have seen. Now thou, O Belteshazzar, declare the interpretation thereof, forasmuch as all the wise men of my kingdom are not able to make known unto me the interpretation: but thou art able; for the spirit of the holy gods is in thee.

Once again recognizing the fallibility of his inner circle of advisors the king demands of the master magician who alone possesses the spirit of God that he declare the meaning of the dream.

[19] Then Daniel, whose name was Belteshazzar, was astonied for one hour, and his thoughts troubled him. The king spake, and said, Belteshazzar, let not the dream, or the interpretation thereof, trouble thee. Belteshazzar answered and said, My lord, the dream be to them that hate thee, and the interpretation thereof to thine enemies.

Instantly after the petition of the king Daniel was amazed for "one hour." The word hour occurs only five times in the whole Hebrew Bible. All of these occurrences happen in the book of Daniel after the Babylonian deportation when the Jews came under the influence of Babylonian culture. After trying to comfort his ace magician the prophet informs the king that the interpretation is ominous.

[20] The tree that thou sawest, which grew, and was strong, whose height reached unto the heaven, and the sight thereof to all the earth;

The magnificent kingdom which grew from a sapling is again described as being the umbilical cord between heaven and earth. The author has not yet acknowledged the identity of the kingdom.

[21] Whose leaves were fair, and the fruit thereof much, and in it was meat for all; under which the beasts of the field dwelt, and upon whose branches the fowls of the heaven had their habitation:

The author continues to describe the glory and health of the kingdom and its ability to provide substance for all of its subjects.

[22] It is thou, O king, that art grown and become strong: for thy greatness is grown, and reacheth unto heaven, and thy dominion to the end of the earth.

Finally, the author reveals what the reader suspected all along, that Nebuchadnezzar is symbolically represented as the tree. The fact that the kingdom grew from a sapling may be an inference to the establishment of the Neo-Babylonian Empire by Nebuchadnezzar's father Nabopolassar in 626 BC and the subsequent dominance of his son Nebuchadnezzar's kingdom on the world stage. The growth of the kingdom by Nebuchadnezzar was so astronomical that it encompassed the whole known world.

[23] And whereas the king saw a watcher and an holy one coming down from heaven, and saying, Hew the tree down, and destroy it; yet leave the stump of the roots thereof in the earth, even with a band of iron and brass, in the tender grass of the field; and let it be wet with the dew of heaven, and let his portion be with the beasts of the field, till seven times pass over him;

Daniel repeats that the punishment would be imminent incarceration among the beasts of the field for a seven-year period with the anticipation of rehabilitation.

[24] This is the interpretation, O king, and this is the decree of the most High, which is come upon my lord the king:

The prophet is compelled to remind the head of gold that the sentence came from the court of the Most High God and cannot be changed.

[25] That they shall drive thee from men, and thy dwelling shall be with the beasts of the field, and they shall make thee to eat grass as oxen, and they shall wet thee with the dew of heaven, and seven times shall pass over thee, till thou know that the most High ruleth in the kingdom of men, and giveth it to whomsoever he will.

Daniel is not specific, but it is likely that once the king's inner court of advisors recognizes his madness they are the ones who will remove him from his throne by force. In order to save any honor, the king has the hierarchy would likely contain and conceal the king as he roams like a beast within the high walls of the inner palace for the seven-year sentence until he recognizes that the discipline of the Most High has been effective.

[26] And whereas they commanded to leave the stump of the tree roots; thy kingdom shall be sure unto thee, after that thou shalt have known that the heavens do rule.

A promise is made to the king that while he is serving his judicial sentence the Neo-Babylonian kingdom will remain in his control, though neither the author nor archaeology reveals who reigned as "coregent".

[27] Wherefore, O king, let my counsel be acceptable unto thee, and break off thy sins by righteousness, and thine iniquities by shewing mercy to the poor; if it may be a lengthening of thy tranquillity.

This is the zenith of Daniel's dialogue before the king. The prophet beseeches the king to hearken unto his council and break off the chains of sin which have entangled him and to do justly. It is an abomination to kings to commit wickedness: for the throne is established by righteousness (Proverbs 16:12). Daniel is not imploring the king that a change of his social policies will perhaps save him from his day of reckoning, but only a change of heart.

[28] All this came upon the king Nebuchadnezzar.

All that the Most High God hath spoken he will do.

[29] At the end of twelve months he walked in the palace of the kingdom of Babylon.

The Babylonian calendar began in March/April and consisted of twelve months with 30 days in each month. The Babylonian calendar was apparently adopted in Israel after the Babylonian conquest as many of the Hebrew month names began to correspond to the Babylonian calendar such as Kislimu/Kislev and Addaru/Adar. The king was literally walking upon or above his palace, that is to say he was walking upon the roof of his palace. The 4th century AD church historian Eusebius quotes a now lost work by the 3rd century BC Greek historian Megasthenes who wrote that Nebuchadnezzar "having ascended to the roof of his palace became inspired (possessed) by some god."

[30] The king spake, and said, Is not this great Babylon, that I have built for the house of the kingdom by the might of my power, and for the honour of my majesty?

The so called East India house foundation tablet (on display at the British Museum) dating from the reign of Nebuchadnezzar which describes the religious devotion and building works of the king similarly states "may the temple I have built endure for all time and may I be satisfied with its splendor."

[31] While the word was in the king's mouth, there fell a voice from heaven, saying, O king Nebuchadnezzar, to thee it is spoken; The kingdom is departed from thee.

Like Herod Agrippa the 1st some 600 years later (Acts 12:21-22), as soon as blasphemy entered Nebuchadnezzar's heart, he was judged by the Most High.

[32] And they shall drive thee from men, and thy dwelling shall be with the beasts of the field: they shall make thee to eat grass as oxen, and seven times shall pass over thee, until thou know that the most High ruleth in the kingdom of men, and giveth it to whomsoever he will.

The voice from heaven repeats verbatim the condemning words of Daniel the prophet (4:25).

[33] The same hour was the thing fulfilled upon Nebuchadnezzar: and he was driven from men, and did eat grass as oxen, and his body was wet with the dew of heaven, till his hairs were grown like eagles' feathers, and his nails like birds' claws.

The medical term for this form of insanity is called boanthropy (ox-man). In 1946 Dr. Raymond Harrison of Britain recorded his experiences of observing a modern-day case of boanthropy. Harrison observed that the patient's only physical abnormality was the lengthening of his hair and a thickened condition of the nails. The patient also spent the entire day outside from dusk till dawn eating handfuls of grass. The king's heart is in the hand of the LORD, as the rivers of water: he turneth it whithersover he will (Proverbs 21:1).

[34] And at the end of the days I Nebuchadnezzar lifted up mine eyes unto heaven, and mine understanding returned unto me, and I blessed the most High, and I praised and honoured him that liveth for ever, whose dominion is an everlasting dominion, and his kingdom is from generation to generation:

At the end of the seven years sentence the king lifts up his eyes, a figurative expression for seeking the help of the Most High (Psalm 123:1). Perhaps the Most High is challenging Nabu the god of Babylon, his namesake who was purportedly the god of wisdom or understanding. Nevertheless, the king's faculties were fully restored and a song of praise to the Most High ensues. There may be an archeological clue that alludes to the time period of Nebuchadnezzar's madness. Assyriologist A.K. Grayson published a cuneiform tablet (on display at the British Museum) that states "his life appeared of no value" and that he continually gave contradictory orders, could not recognize his own family members, or contribute in any of his building projects. Some commentators have also suggested that there is evidence that the Babylonian military did not partake in any military operations during this seven-year period.

[35] And all the inhabitants of the earth are reputed as nothing: and he doeth according to his will in the army of heaven, and among the inhabitants of the earth: and none can stay his hand, or say unto him, What doest thou?

The praise continues by the restored king, acknowledging that mankind is reckoned (*chashab*) as naught by the God of the watchers. The terms heaven and earth are used in opposition to express the totality of the Most High's domain. The hand of God is often portrayed in the Scriptures as both a positive (Ecclesiastes 2:24) and negative (Job 19:21) extension of his will.

[36] At the same time my reason returned unto me; and for the glory of my kingdom, mine honour and brightness returned unto me; and my counsellers and my lords sought unto me; and I was established in my kingdom, and excellent majesty was added unto me.

In opposition to when his boastful words left his mouth and his insanity instantly struck, now, when his words of confession and praise left his lips, his glory was instantaneously restored unto him. The important ranks of his advisors once again held appointments with him and the king was even greater than he was before.

[37] Now I Nebuchadnezzar praise and extol and honour the King of heaven, all whose works are truth, and his ways judgment: and those that walk in pride he is able to abase.

The chapter ends the same way it began, with the king speaking in the first person and flourishing in his palace. The great king did not live long after the events of this narrative. In fact, this is the last time the king is mentioned in the book as being alive. Nevertheless, his last recorded words are those of praise and to the Most High God and admonition to prideful men.

Daniel 5

[1] Belshazzar the king made a great feast to a thousand of his lords, and drank wine before the thousand.

The chapter begins with the introduction of the last king of the Neo Babylonian-Empire; Belshazzar whose name means "Bel protect the king." Some have suggested that Bel is a title instead of a proper name and was especially used of Marduk. The events of chapter five take place in 539 BC, some 30 years after the events of chapter four. After the death of Nebuchadnezzar, the following Babylonian kings were Evil Merodach (562-560), Neriglissar (560-556), Labashi Marduk (556), Nabonidus (556-539), and then finally the subordinate king Belshazzar (553-539). Belshazzar was considered a crown prince because he was left in control of the kingdom while his father Nabonidus was on a four-year military campaign in Arabia. Since Belshazzar wasn't an "official king" and administered under the authority of his father, the king Nabonidus, later Greek writers were not interested in making a deliberate effort to preserve his name. Nevertheless, once again an archeological object confirms the Biblical text. In 1861 H.F. Talbot published Babylonian cuneiform tablets found at the Moon Temple one of which contained a prayer dedicated by Belshazzar. In 1882, Professor Theophilus Pinches published the "Nabonidus Chronicle" which mentions Belshazzar and places him as an equal to his father as a Babylonian official. Again in 1924 Sidney Smith of the British Museum published the investigation of the "Persian Verse Account of Nabonidus" which states that Nabonidus entrusted the kingship to Belshazzar. In the tradition of ANE kings, Belshazzar hosted a great feast. The strength and glory of a king was often reflected in the magnitude of these parties. In 869 B.C., the Assyrian king Ashurnasirpal II celebrated the completion of his palace at Kalhu by hosting a banquet of 69,574 guests. The wedding of Alexander the Great to one of his multiple wives took place in Susa and was attended by 10,000 guests. No reason is given for the reason for the state banquet, but a Midrashic interpretation states that Belshazzar miscalculated the 70-year prophecy of Jeremiah and threw a party to commemorate the inaccuracy of the prophecy.

[2] Belshazzar, whiles he tasted the wine, commanded to bring the golden and silver vessels which his father Nebuchadnezzar had taken out of the temple which was in Jerusalem; that the king, and his princes, his wives, and his concubines, might drink therein.

In the midst of his drunken stupor the king commands for the holy vessels taken from Jerusalem, which were likely stored in the Temple of Belus, to be brought forth. It may be possible that the king is celebrating his miscalculation of the 70-year prophecy by drinking from the cups of the city centered in the prophecy of Jeremiah. The author of the book of kings mentions these exact vessels in his list of items taken from Jerusalem by his "father" Nebuchadnezzar (2 Kings 24:13). There is no Hebrew word for "father" and history tells us that there were four kings between Nebuchadnezzar and Belshazzar so we are to understand "father" to include the meanings of grandfather, great grandfather, etc. It is possible that Belshazzar was Nebuchadnezzar's grandson as Jeremiah prophesied that "all nations shall serve him (Nebuchadnezzar), and his son, and his son's son, until the very time of his land come" (Jeremiah 27:7).

[3] Then they brought the golden vessels that were taken out of the temple of the house of God which was at Jerusalem; and the king, and his princes, his wives, and his concubines, drank in them.

Ezra tells us that there were exactly 5,400 vessels taken from Jerusalem by Nebuchadnezzar (Ezra 1:11). These vessels were the sacred containers used in the worship of YHWH in Jerusalem but were now being put on display to symbolize the conquered status of the Jews. The vessels were the only material link the Jews had between the Temple of Solomon and the future hope of a second temple.

[4] They drank wine, and praised the gods of gold, and of silver, of brass, of iron, of wood, and of stone.

The art of metallurgy for ornament or weapons can be traced back to the 7th from Adam; Tubalcain through the line of Cain (Gen. 4:22). Tools, utensils, and ornaments of bronze have been found among Egyptian and Assyrian remains. The vessels of the Tabernacle were probably either copper or bronze – but represented as brass – but some of the vessels of the Temple were made of gold and silver. Brass is compounded of copper and zinc and is said to be of a later date than the era of the written Word. Nebuchadnezzar his father had great respect or maybe superstition for the sanctity of these vessels to have them stored in the temple treasury but his despicable son and the other hierarchy of this drunken orgy blasphemed the Most High God.

[5] In the same hour came forth fingers of a man's hand, and wrote over against the candlestick upon the plaister of the wall of the king's palace: and the king saw the part of the hand that wrote.

The writing took place on plaster, often a mixed lime, sand and water substance applied to stone walls that would almost sparkle when finished. The writing took place opposite of a lamp stand in order to advertise the writing on the wall. Some have suggested that this candlestick or lamp stand was the same instrument taken from the Temple in Jerusalem. Just as it does not mention anyone else seeing the fourth man in the furnace so the author doesn't mention anyone else seeing the hand that wrote the message. Interestingly, archaeologists have found a throne room in the palace of Nebuchadnezzar that was 56-foot-wide and 173 feet long that had plastered walls and was possibly the setting for this scene.

[6] Then the king's countenance was changed, and his thoughts troubled him, so that the joints of his loins were loosed, and his knees smote one against another.

The superstitious king likely thought the miracle was a vindication of the holiness of the Most High God and his vessels. So terrified was the king that the color went from his face and his legs gave way. This is a common ancient description to express terror (Nahum 2:10).

[7] The king cried aloud to bring in the astrologers, the Chaldeans, and the soothsayers. And the king spake, and said to the wise men of Babylon, Whosoever shall read this writing, and shew me the interpretation thereof, shall be clothed with scarlet, and have a chain of gold about his neck, and shall be the third ruler in the kingdom.

With a loud proclaim the king summoned the guilds of magi and offered the highest possible position to the man who could solve the riddle. Indeed, we have a clue in this verse that confirms the archeological account of Belshazzar being the crown prince. The reason the coregent can only offer the third position and not the second is because he himself is second in command while his father was on a military expedition in Arabia.

[8] Then came in all the king's wise men: but they could not read the writing, nor make known to the king the interpretation thereof.

The reason the magi could not read the writing was because the message was an anagram written in Aramaic. That is not to say the magi couldn't read Aramaic, certainly they were versed in the *lingua franca* but this wordplay rearranged the letters of the words to produce a new word that stumped them from interpreting the writing.

[9] Then was king Belshazzar greatly troubled, and his countenance was changed in him, and his lords were astonied.

This is the first recognition by the author that Belshazzar was indeed the king or crown prince. Upon notification that all the wise men of Babylon could not solve the puzzle his brightness dimmed and splendor faded which greatly startled his political allies.

[10] Now the queen, by reason of the words of the king and his lords, came into the banquet house: and the queen spake and said, O king, live for ever: let not thy thoughts trouble thee, nor let thy countenance be changed:

The identification of the queen is an enigma. Some have suggested that the queen is none other than the aged widow of Nebuchadnezzar, Amytis of Media. The marriage of Amytis to Nebuchadnezzar concreted the union of the empires of Babylon and Media during the Neo-Babylonian Empire. Legend has it that the construction of the Hanging Gardens of Babylon by Nebuchadnezzar was to relive her homesickness for the forested mountains of the Median Empire. Another possibility is that the queen could have been Belshazzar's mother, Nitocris, the daughter of Nebuchadnezzar.

[11] There is a man in thy kingdom, in whom is the spirit of the holy gods; and in the days of thy father light and understanding and wisdom, like the wisdom of the gods, was found in him; whom the king Nebuchadnezzar thy father, the king, I say, thy father, made master of the magicians, astrologers, Chaldeans, and soothsayers;

What is clear is this person was either not invited to the banquet or deliberately chose not to partake in the blasphemy. She was calm, dignified and sure of who was the solution to the king's predicament. Evidently the queen was knowledgeable about the ministry and the God of the prophet Daniel and Belshazzar was not – even though Daniel was from within his own court. We are interested in what we want to be interested in and not interested in what we do not want to be interested in. The spiritual ignorance of men of distinction can be alarming, as, in like manner, King Saul had never heard of the prophet Samuel (1 Samuel 9:6-21). It is also possible that Daniel was demoted from his high position after the death of Nebuchadnezzar.

[12] Forasmuch as an excellent spirit, and knowledge, and understanding, interpreting of dreams, and shewing of hard sentences, and dissolving of doubts, were found in the same Daniel, whom the king named Belteshazzar: now let Daniel be called, and he will shew the interpretation.

The queen continues to praise Belteshazzar, whom she recognizes by his Hebrew name, Daniel. She recognizes Daniel as having gifts from the gods and that he alone as the master magician can dissolve the doubt or solve the difficult problem of the king.

[13] Then was Daniel brought in before the king. And the king spake and said unto Daniel, Art thou that Daniel, which art of the children of the captivity of Judah, whom the king my father brought out of Jewry?

Once again Daniel enters the scene after all the magi of Babylon fail. Interestingly the king addresses Daniel by his Hebrew name. This could be out of spite because the names Belteshazzar and Belshazzar are very similar, and also because of the fact that they were possibly just celebrating the miscalculated failing of the 70-year prophecy of the Jews. The queen introduced Daniel as the wise man of Babylon, where the depraved king reminds the prophet that he came to Babylon as a prisoner of war. Having just put Daniel in his place the crown prince reminds the prophet of his affinity with the famous Nebuchadnezzar.

[14] I have even heard of thee, that the spirit of the gods is in thee, and that light and understanding and excellent wisdom is found in thee.

Possibly just hearing about the famous prophet for the first-time moments ago and after seemingly putting him in his place the king praises Daniel, knowing that he would need his extraordinary wisdom to solve the supernatural riddle.

[15] And now the wise men, the astrologers, have been brought in before me, that they should read this writing, and make known unto me the interpretation thereof: but they could not shew the interpretation of the thing:

This predicament was nothing new to Daniel as Belshazzar's "father," for Nebuchadnezzar was in the same dilemma and also summoned Daniel after his own magi failed.

[16] And I have heard of thee, that thou canst make interpretations, and dissolve doubts: now if thou canst read the writing, and make known to me the interpretation thereof, thou shalt be clothed with scarlet, and have a chain of gold about thy neck, and shalt be the third ruler in the kingdom.

Like Joseph, the Hebrew prophets in whom is the Spirit of God rise through the ranks of the Gentile world system to glorify the Most High God as the only true and living God. Belshazzar almost exactly echoes the words of Pharaoh while commanding the prophet to interpret the meaning (Genesis 41:14) and then offers him the same reward (Genesis 41:42).

[17] Then Daniel answered and said before the king, Let thy gifts be to thyself, and give thy rewards to another; yet I will read the writing unto the king, and make known to him the interpretation.

Like his exalted father (Abraham) Daniel refuses to take any gifts from the hand of a wicked and pagan Gentile king (Genesis 14:21-24). Nevertheless, in order to glorify the Most High God and honor His recently desecrated holy vessels, Daniel decides to interpret the dream.

[18] O thou king, the most high God gave Nebuchadnezzar thy father a kingdom, and majesty, and glory, and honour:

Out of respect for the placing of the king by the hand of God, Daniel recognizes Belshazzar as king despite his vile conduct toward the Temple treasures. Daniel begins his discourse by reminding Belshazzar that Daniel's God, the Most High God, gave the dominion he now oversees to his "father" Nebuchadnezzar.

[19] And for the majesty that he gave him, all people, nations, and languages, trembled and feared before him: whom he would he slew; and whom he would he kept alive; and whom he would he set up; and whom he would he put down.

The authority given to Nebuchadnezzar was so terrible that the whole known world shuddered at his military and political presence. An apt description of the unpredictable nature of the head of gold is here described, a dictator with supreme power to do what he decided instantaneously.

[20] But when his heart was lifted up, and his mind hardened in pride, he was deposed from his kingly throne, and they took his glory from him:

Daniel reminds the king of the events that took place in chapter four some 30 years before, possibly preparing the king for the ominous news that his heart too is hardened with pride and he must also be deposed by the Most High God.

[21] And he was driven from the sons of men; and his heart was made like the beasts, and his dwelling was with the wild asses: they fed him with grass like oxen, and his body was wet with the dew of heaven; till he knew that the most high God ruled in the kingdom of men, and that he appointeth over it whomsoever he will.

The prophet uses parallelism by describing Nebuchadnezzar's lifted up heart with his condemned state of having the heart of a beast. He reminds the king that Nebuchadnezzar lifted up his eyes to heaven, that is to say, he sought the help of the Most High God, humbled his heart and was restored to his throne.

[22] And thou his son, O Belshazzar, hast not humbled thine heart, though thou knewest all this;

Belshazzar is here called the son of Nebuchadnezzar. The word "son" can mean a successor to the throne as in the Black Obelisk of Shalmaneser II where Israel's King Jehu is called the Son of Omri, even though Jehu was not related and was actually a usurper of the throne (2 Kings 9). Though Belshazzar knew of Nebuchadnezzar's misfortune and possibly even saw the king in his animal like state as a young boy, and even heard the king or heard of the restored king's praises to the Most High God – whose vessels he desecrated – he, like Pharaoh, hardened his heart to the Most High.

[23] But hast lifted up thyself against the Lord of heaven; and they have brought the vessels of his house before thee, and thou, and thy lords, thy wives, and thy concubines, have drunk wine in them; and thou hast praised the gods of silver, and gold, of brass, iron, wood, and stone, which see not, nor hear, nor know: and the God in whose hand thy breath is, and whose are all thy ways, hast thou not glorified:

This is the only time in the Hebrew Bible where the designation "Lord of heaven" is used. Daniel informs the king that the reason the Lord of heaven will destroy him and his kingdom was the desecration of the sacred Temple treasures. No pardon would be available for the king, in contrast to his "father," for he openly and defiantly rejected the message God gave through Nebuchadnezzar and defiled the same God's holiest things.

[24] Then was the part of the hand sent from him; and this writing was written.

The same hand of God that wrote the Ten Commandments (Exodus 31:18) and restored his "father" is the same hand Belshazzar bit.

[25] And this is the writing that was written, MENE, MENE, TEKEL, UPHARSIN.

The doomed king is now given what he wanted all along; the interpretation of the foreboding supernatural Aramaic message. It is possible that the words were written in consonantal form (without vowels) and appeared without word divisions which compounded the difficulty of their interpretation for the magi. The English transliteration may have appeared as MN'MN' TKLPRS.

[26] This is the interpretation of the thing: MENE; God hath numbered thy kingdom, and finished it.

The first two words are repeated twice to emphasize their meaning. The Aramaic word *mene* has a double meaning and can mean to number or to fix the limit. The days of the Babylonian kingdom have been numbered or reached their bounds that they cannot pass. This reminds us of the Amorites who dwelt in the land of Canaan until their iniquity was full (Genesis 15:16).

[27] TEKEL; Thou art weighed in the balances, and art found wanting.

The third Aramaic word, *tekel*, means to weigh. Belshazzar has been weighed in the scales and found deficient. Men are weighed by the Most High God to determine their degrees of reward or punishment (1 Samuel 2:3).

[28] PERES; Thy kingdom is divided, and given to the Medes and Persians.

The fourth Aramaic word *peres* means to divide. The Babylonian kingdom would be taken over by a dual monarchy, the Medes and Persians with emphasis given to the Persian Empire. The word *peres* that appeared on the wall in the original text did not have vowels and was identical to the Aramaic word for Persian, *paras*.

[29] Then commanded Belshazzar, and they clothed Daniel with scarlet, and put a chain of gold about his neck, and made a proclamation concerning him, that he should be the third ruler in the kingdom.

True to his word, the doomed king publicly honored Daniel and in order to save face presented Daniel the promised gifts though Daniel had previously rejected them. Belshazzar also reestablished him to his possible demoted position to once again being the next in line to rule and reign Babylon.

[30] In that night was Belshazzar the king of the Chaldeans slain.

The Scriptures do not tell us the details of the events that transpired with the death of the king and subsequent overthrow of the short lived Neo-Babylonian Empire. The Nabonidus Chronicle tells us that Babylon and its great empire fell into the hands of the Persians in the course of the same night, October 12, 539 BC. While the attention of the city was drawn towards Belshazzar's feast, the Persians diverted a portion of the Euphrates River and its soldiers were able to maneuver underneath the gated passageways through which the river flowed and into the walled city of Babylon. This account is elaborated on by the Greek historian Herodotus (1:191).

[31] And Darius the Median took the kingdom, being about threescore and two years old.

This rulers name was Gubaru and "Darius" was his title which means "the holder of the scepter." He was a might subordinate to Cyrus the Great "which was made king over the realm of the Chaldeans" (Daniel 9:1). The Nabonidus Chronicle informs us that once Belshazzar's father Nabonidus returned from his military expedition he was arrested and once the city was at peace Cyrus the Great entered Babylon as the inhabitants laid green branches at his feet. After Cyrus sent his best wishes to the city the tablet goes on to say Darius "installed sub-governors in Babylon" (Daniel 6:1).

Daniel 6

[1] It pleased Darius to set over the kingdom an hundred and twenty princes, which should be over the whole kingdom;

Darius, whose title means "the holder of the scepter" is known historically as Gubaru. As previously noted he was subordinate to Cyrus the Great and the Nabondius Chronicle declares that Darius "installed sub-governors in Babylon" which the biblical account confirms in this verse. The territory under the authority of the Medo-Persian Empire was significantly larger than the previous Babylonian Empire. The Medo-Persian Empire included not only all of the conquered Babylonian territory but all of modern day Iran, into western India, all of modern day Turkey and across the Mediterranean Sea into Greece. These 120 appointed satraps were high administrative governors under the authority of the empire who ruled over a large province or even a small populace. It is difficult to pinpoint the date of the events in the chapter but it was probably in 539 BC or shortly thereafter, once the Medo-Persians had stabilized the region.

[2] And over these three presidents; of whom Daniel was first: that the princes might give accounts unto them, and the king should have no damage.

Darius also appointed three magistrates or overseers (*carek*) in the chain of command who would report to them and they would report to Darius so he would "suffer no loss." A possible reading can mean that the king can collect taxes in an organized fashion. It was common for ANE kings to have counselors in their company to report on current events; Artaxerxes the king of Persia had seven counselors (Ezra 7:14). Interestingly the chapter does not mention Daniel's Babylonian name Belteshazzar, since the events in the chapter are based in a Medo-Persian setting.

[3] Then this Daniel was preferred above the presidents and princes, because an excellent spirit was in him; and the king thought to set him over the whole realm.

Like Nebuchadnezzar, who recognized the brilliant character of Daniel, so Darius after an undisclosed time does the same and contemplates promoting Daniel to chief governor or third in command. Undoubtedly Darius was informed of Daniel's previous position as second in command of Babylon and this likely influenced his decision. Similarly, Jeremiah the prophet was honored by Nebuchadnezzar after he heard of his words and works and offered for him to live comfortably in Babylon or serve in an honored position in the defeated region of Judah (Jeremiah 40:1-6).

[4] Then the presidents and princes sought to find occasion against Daniel concerning the kingdom; but they could find none occasion nor fault; forasmuch as he was faithful, neither was there any error or fault found in him.

Jealous of the aged prophet's influence and prominence, the Gentile princes plotted to exercise dominion and remove Daniel from his conduct in the governments affairs – but came away empty handed, finding no evidence of corruption (*shechath*) or bribes. Daniel's characteristic of being faithful (*aman*) comes from the same root as the Hebrew word for "Amen."

[5] Then said these men, We shall not find any occasion against this Daniel, except we find it against him concerning the law of his God.

Since Daniel had a renowned clean testimony the only way to entrap the prophet was to pit his devotion to the Torah (instruction) of his God against the law of the Medo-Persian Empire. The devotion to the Torah would include dietary restrictions (Daniel 1), not lying, (Daniel 2) not bowing down to idols (Daniel 3), a clean heart (Daniel 4), and not consuming strong drink (Daniel 5).

[6] Then these presidents and princes assembled together to the king, and said thus unto him, King Darius, live for ever.

The anti-Semitic administrators now swarmed together in the throne room of Darius to pitch their ill-conceived campaign against the third in command of the Medo-Persian Empire, and acknowledged Darius with the flattering yet customary ANE monarchial greeting.

[7] All the presidents of the kingdom, the governors, and the princes, the counsellers, and the captains, have consulted together to establish a royal statute, and to make a firm decree, that whosoever shall ask a petition of any God or man for thirty days, save of thee, O king, he shall be cast into the den of lions.

The partial truth of their narrative seemed plausible to the king in light of Persian king's religious tolerance and the renowned haughtiness and egos of ANE emperors. The well known pharaoh-worshiping of the Egyptians (and the soon to come god-man worship of Alexander the Great) was attractive enough to deceive the king in a moment of weakness. The penalty for beseeching any god rather than Darius for the month was apparently the standard form of execution in the Medo-Persian Empire, the lion's den, whereas Nebuchadnezzar's was death by fire. The Medo-Persians rejected this form of execution, likely because many were Zoroastrians who worshiped Atar, the god of holy fire.

[8] Now, O king, establish the decree, and sign the writing, that it be not changed, according to the law of the Medes and Persians, which altereth not.

Knowing the irreversibility of Medo-Persian policies the wicked administrators seemingly had finally conquered Daniel the prophet. The silver arms of the Medo-Persian Empire were weaker in value than the head of gold that was the Babylonian Empire. Nebuchadnezzar the dictator's form of government operated on his word and his word alone and could be amended or deleted at his bidding, unlike the current government. An extra biblical account that parallels this form of Medo-Persian policy making is found in the 1st century BC book *Historical Library* (17.5.3-6.3) by Diodorus of Sicily. The historian writes of an event during the reign of the 4th century BC Medo-Persian king Darius III, who in haste ordered the execution of Charidemus. But upon further reflection "he at once repented...and it was not possible for what was done by the royal authority to be undone."

[9] Wherefore king Darius signed the writing and the decree.

ANE kings were susceptible to rash decisions which later ensnared them in a terrible dilemma. Examples are David, who wrote a letter to smite Uriah (2 Samuel 11:15), and Herod, who executed John the Baptist (Matthew 14:9).

[10] Now when Daniel knew that the writing was signed, he went into his house; and his windows being open in his chamber toward Jerusalem, he kneeled upon his knees three times a day, and prayed, and gave thanks before his God, as he did aforetime.

He did not orient himself to the sun, as the Zoroastrians (Ezek. 8:16), but towards the Holy Jerusalem where the Temple once stood. This was a custom of the Jews (1 Kings 8:44, Psalm 5:7, Jonah 2:4). There is no internal biblical evidence for a set time of Jewish prayers, so it seems that Daniel oriented his prayer time in accordance with the morning and evening sacrificial system of the destroyed Jerusalem Temple. To this he apparently added a noon prayer (Psalm 55:17). Daniel did not wait for a calamity to petition the Most High God.

[11] Then these men assembled, and found Daniel praying and making supplication before his God.

Surmising that Daniel would not hearken unto Darius more than he would to his God, the assailants seemingly caught Daniel red-handed. Those who wished to "find fault" with the prophet now "find him praying."

[12] Then they came near, and spake before the king concerning the king's decree; Hast thou not signed a decree, that every man that shall ask a petition of any God or man within thirty days, save of thee, O king, shall be cast into the den of lions? The king answered and said, The thing is true, according to the law of the Medes and Persians, which altereth not.

Instantly the accusers thronged the throne room to inform the king that his right-hand man had defied the king himself by breaking the very law he had just initiated. Whereas Daniel petitions his God these men petition the king. The term "den of lions" is a bit misleading. The word for den (*gob*) means pit. The pit was likely a deep hand dug cistern which was sealed on the mouth or the top of the cavity with a stone. Lion hunting was an infamous hobby of ANE kings, many of which likely ended up as trophies or killing machines in such pits.

[13] Then answered they and said before the king, That Daniel, which is of the children of the captivity of Judah, regardeth not thee, O king, nor the decree that thou hast signed, but maketh his petition three times a day.

Like Belshazzar (Daniel 5:13) these administrators attempt to diminish Daniel by portraying him as a prisoner of war and rebellious Jew who, like his countrymen, defied Nebuchadnezzar. The accusers of the Hebrews at the burning fiery furnace brought the same charges as these officials (Daniel 3:12). In this moment of crisis, the reader is reminded of the miracles of the Most High God when he so chooses and gives hope that Daniel too will be delivered.

[14] Then the king, when he heard these words, was sore displeased with himself, and set his heart on Daniel to deliver him: and he laboured till the going down of the sun to deliver him.

Like the extra-biblical account of Diodorus of Sicily who records the repentance of Darius III and his impotence to reverse the law, so Darius (Gubaru) does the same, once he recognizes the real reason for the hasty decree. Apparently, there was a Medo-Persian law that criminals must be executed post-haste.

[15] Then these men assembled unto the king, and said unto the king, Know, O king, that the law of the Medes and Persians is, That no decree nor statute which the king establisheth may be changed.

The court etiquette should be compared to Esther 1:19. Here the expression "Medes and Persians" is used, the Medes preceding the later because Darius is being addressed. In Esther, the order is reversed because Ahasuerus was a Persian.

[16] Then the king commanded, and they brought Daniel, and cast him into the den of lions. Now the king spake and said unto Daniel, Thy God whom thou servest continually, he will deliver thee.

Just as the Hebrews were thrown into the furnace in the presence of the king, so Daniel is thrown into the pit in the presence of the king. The Medo-Persian Empire - which had an affinity for executing criminals the same day they were apprehended – took Daniel and cast him headlong to his supposed death. Likely an unusual form of etiquette the king attended the execution of the state criminal and more literally said "May your (God) deliver thee." This was not the king's God - who happened to be Ahura Mazda the uncreated spirit of Zoroastrianism. The king is expressing that the God of Daniel will deliver him since the king himself was incapable of doing so.

[17] And a stone was brought and laid upon the mouth of the den; and the king sealed it with his own signet, and with the signet of his lords; that the purpose might not be changed concerning Daniel.

In order to seal the tomb from someone attempting to rescue Daniel, the government fastened the pit and, with cords wrapped around the stone, impressed the king's and his lord's seal onto the clay or wax or whatever substance was used to ensure the seal (Matthew 27:66). Interestingly the seal was also sealed by the administrators of Darius, the king possibly not trusting them to interfere with the king's decree so he also sealed it himself. In the ANE seals functioned for a variety of purposes. Generally speaking they were the equivalent of our wallet. Your identification would be needed in order to purchase something of significance, pay taxes, send letters, or provide a number of functions for the government. The Song of Solomon mentions that seals were often worn on chains around the neck or placed in an armlet to ensure safety and easy access (Song of Solomon 8:6). Many of the signets of ANE kings portrayed them involved in heroic feats with a representation of their choice deity. Since the signet ring is as close to the king as you can physically get, the prophet Haggai mentions Zerubbabel's (meaning "sown or born in Babel") exalted position in the kingdom as a signet (Haggai 2:23).

[18] Then the king went to his palace, and passed the night fasting: neither were instruments of musick brought before him: and his sleep went from him.

With nothing more, the king could do he departed to the former palace of Nebuchadnezzar, now the headquarters of the Medo-Persian nobility or more likely the great royal architect went to the temple of his chief deity. The word *heykal* can mean palace or temple. Darius abstained from the richest meal of the day (Exodus 16:8) and in a state of mourning had no need for his normal evening leisure. It is easy to see the parallel of a sleepless night between Darius and later his son Xerxes the son of Atossa the daughter of Cyrus the Great (Esther 6:1).

[19] Then the king arose very early in the morning, and went in haste unto the den of lions.
At the crack of dawn the king, having been up all night, left the temple or palace and quickly went to inquire of Daniel, just as the women who followed the Lord did (Mark 16:2). Throughout the Scriptures there are numerous occasions where one wakes very early in the morning to fulfill an urgent task (Genesis 19:27, 20:8, 31:55, Exodus 8:20, etc.).

[20] And when he came to the den, he cried with a lamentable voice unto Daniel: and the king spake and said to Daniel, O Daniel, servant of the living God, is thy God, whom thou servest continually, able to deliver thee from the lions?
Possibly the king brought his bodyguards to break the seal and remove the stone. Nevertheless, he cried with

anguish to see if Daniel was delivered like his Hebrew friends had been. Addressing his God as "the living God," the king was certainly familiar with the pure and undefiled religion of the prophet.

[21] Then said Daniel unto the king, O king, live for ever.

Daniel here addresses the king in the customary and respectable ANE fashion.

[22] My God hath sent his angel, and hath shut the lions' mouths, that they have not hurt me: forasmuch as before him innocency was found in me; and also before thee, O king, have I done no hurt.

The same messenger or angel who delivered Daniel's Hebrew friends from the fiery furnace (Daniel 3:28) delivers the prophet from the lions. It is as if the lions ate straw like the oxen (Isaiah 11:7). For the first time in the narrative Daniel proclaims his blamelessness in regards to breaking the king's law and reveals he had no ill intentions against the king himself. The king could shut the mouth of the den but only God can shut the lion's mouth.

[23] Then was the king exceeding glad for him, and commanded that they should take Daniel up out of the den. So Daniel was taken up out of the den, and no manner of hurt was found upon him, because he believed in his God.

Overjoyed, the king hastened to have Daniel removed from the pit and all saw that "by faith the lion's mouths were stopped" (Hebrews 11:33) like all previously saw that "by faith they quenched the violence of fire" (Hebrews 11:34).

[24] And the king commanded, and they brought those men which had accused Daniel, and they cast them into the den of lions, them, their children, and their wives; and the lions had the mastery of them, and brake all their bones in pieces or ever they came at the bottom of the den.

The lions devoured everyone and everything including their bones. In ANE custom not only were those responsible for their crime executed but also, by association, the families were killed as well (Joshua 7:15-26). Among other reasons this was to quench any future descendents from seeking revenge on the king for the death of their father. A similar account of corporate family punishment by Darius is mentioned by Herodotus (The Histories 3:119).

[25] Then king Darius wrote unto all people, nations, and languages, that dwell in all the earth; Peace be multiplied unto you.

Like Nebuchadnezzar, whom God gave authority over all the earth, so now the shoulders of silver have been given dominion over all the known earth. Also like Nebuchadnezzar (Daniel 4:1) who had witnessed a miracle by the Most High God and sent a testimony of shalom or peace to the world, so Darius does the same.

[26] I make a decree, That in every dominion of my kingdom men tremble and fear before the God of Daniel: for he is the living God, and stedfast for ever, and his kingdom that which shall not be destroyed, and his dominion shall be even unto the end.

An unchangeable decree like the decree to cast Daniel into the pit is now proclaimed throughout the empire. The decree is for all to revere the God of the Jews as the living God and supreme over the kingdom, in comparison to the idols of wood, silver, and stone which neither see, nor hear, nor walk, whose power was thought to have been contained within the boundaries of the kingdom they were worshiped.

[27] He delivereth and rescueth, and he worketh signs and wonders in heaven and in earth, who hath delivered Daniel from the power of the lions.

The king continues his praise and proclamation centered on the God of the Jews by recognizing the Living God as the only deity capable of the kind of supernatural intervention the king had just witnessed.

[28] So this Daniel prospered in the reign of Darius, and in the reign of Cyrus the Persian.

Daniel continued to minister in the government of the Medo-Persian Empire as third in command under Darius (or Gubaru) who was himself subordinate to Cyrus the Great until his dying day.

Daniel 7

[1] In the first year of Belshazzar king of Babylon Daniel had a dream and visions of his head upon his bed: then he wrote the dream, and told the sum of the matters.

The system of chapter divisions was introduced in 1258 by Cardinal Hugo de Sicaro and verse notations were added in 1551 by Robertus Stephanus after the advent of the printing press. The second half of Daniel, unlike the first half which was predominately narrative or historical, is predominately prophetic or apocalyptic in nature. The second half of the book begins with four prophetic visions which primarily emphasize the destiny of Israel among the nations. Because of the chronological peg given in the verse we can date the book to the first year of the reign of the last king (crown prince) of the Neo-Babylonian Empire, Belshazzar, in 553 BC. Close to 50 years has now passed since Daniel interpreted the end times dream for king Nebuchadnezzar, who has been dead for about 10 years.

[2] Daniel spake and said, I saw in my vision by night, and, behold, the four winds of the heaven strove upon the great sea.

Apparently as soon as he arose the prophet put ink to parchment to record what appeared (*chezev*) during the night watch. The word behold (*'aruw*) is often used as a literary device in order to reel in the attention of the reader to an extraordinary message. The first thing Daniel records seeing are the four winds or the four points of the compass. Sargon of Akkad, who ruled shortly before the birth of Abraham, was entrusted with kingship over "the four corners of the earth." The energy and power of the cosmos is seen clashing with the sea from all directions. Depending on the context, the sea in Scripture is often representative of fallen humanity or chaos (Revelation 13:1).

[3] And four great beasts came up from the sea, diverse one from another.

To the ancient Hebrews the sea was considered an abode of disorder, instability, and evil. The great dragon lives in the sea (Isaiah 27:1), the wicked are compared to the troubled sea (Isaiah 57:20), the demon possessed swine chose to run into the depths of the sea (Matthew 8:32); therefore, there is no sea in heaven (Revelation

21:1). Out of this chaos and from the depths of humanity arise four distinct and ferocious animals.

[4] The first was like a lion, and had eagle's wings: I beheld till the wings thereof were plucked, and it was lifted up from the earth, and made stand upon the feet as a man, and a man's heart was given to it.

The first creature is depicted as the king of the jungle with the swiftness of an eagle (Jeremiah 49:19, Ezekiel 17:3). The beast's mobility was removed and it was humbled to the earth until a set time passed and a new heart or inner control center made the deprived beast a man. There are many parallels between the second and seventh chapter of Daniel. Both chapters consist of what some call a four plus one prophecy; four distinct empires eventually thrown down by the one God. Unlike chapter two, which describes the empires in the most precious metals known to man, the seventh chapter emphasizes their depravity, cruelty and oppression. Obviously the first beast corresponds to the head of gold, the Neo-Babylonian Empire, with special emphasis given to Nebuchadnezzar who had his pride plucked from him like the eagle had its feathers plucked from his body and who had the spiritual transformation of receiving a new heart.

[5] And behold another beast, a second, like to a bear, and it raised up itself on one side, and it had three ribs in the mouth of it between the teeth of it: and they said thus unto it, Arise, devour much flesh.

In accordance with the second chapter of Daniel another beast or empire follows on the heels of the first. This beast is described as a lopsided bear and is not as majestic as the great lion because one of the shoulders or arms of the beast is given prominence over the other. The raised-up side of the second beast would be the more influential Persian Empire compared to the subordinate Median Empire. The three ribs in the beast's mouth would be the three major empires the bear gobbled up under the reign of Cyrus and his son Cambyses on the way to its zenith. These would be the peoples of Lydia in Asia Minor under King Croesus (546 BC), Babylonia under Belshazzar (539 BC), and Egypt under Psamtik III (525 BC).

[6] After this I beheld, and lo another, like a leopard, which had upon the back of it four wings of a fowl; the beast had also four heads; and dominion was given to it.

The third empire is described as a swift and violent beast of prey, a leopard with four wings to propel its blitzkrieg style and four heads, or distinct divisions of the same empire. In accordance with chapter two the third kingdom, the Greek Empire, upon the death of Alexander the Great (323 BC) was divided into four entities. The four wings were as follows: Casander who ruled over Greece and Macedonia, Lysimachus who ruled over Thrace and Asia Minor, Antigonus (later Seleueus) who ruled over Babylon, India, Syria, etc., and Ptolemy who ruled over Egypt, Israel and Arabia. If Nebuchadnezzar conquered quickly with two wings, Alexander's empire exceeded him doubly.

[7] After this I saw in the night visions, and behold a fourth beast, dreadful and terrible, and strong exceedingly; and it had great iron teeth: it devoured and brake in pieces, and stamped the residue with the feet of it: and it was diverse from all the beasts that were before it; and it had ten horns.

In accordance with the parallel vision in chapter two a fourth empire (Rome) emerges on the scene. The empire is characterized as having a furious and ferocious appetite for carnage. The beast is described as being diverse from all others, likely due to its enormous size and form of government. Daniel can hardly find the words to describe the beast but conveys that the beast breaks everything in its path to pieces and then stomps on whatever remains. The parallels between the two visions continue as the latter government of the statue had ten toes and this final government has ten horns or sources of power, and also the same metallic substance of iron is used to characterize the empire in both accounts. In order to emphasize the message of a dream God will sometimes give a king, or in this case a king and a prophet, two distinct yet similar dreams (Genesis 41:1-7).

[8] I considered the horns, and, behold, there came up among them another little horn, before whom there were three of the first horns plucked up by the roots: and, behold, in this horn were eyes like the eyes of man, and a mouth speaking great things.

From the midst of the yet future revived Roman Empire which seems to be consolidated into ten related units, another horn or person of power will arise. Out of the midst of the ten-horn coalition a mysterious and otherwise unknown person of strength will with lightning speed depose of 30% of the government at that time - analogous to the bear devouring three empires on its current political stage. The so called little horn is characterized as having the eyes of man or great brilliance (Zechariah 3:9, 4:10) and speaking with great yet negative influences despite his little size, but according to this verse his duration of rule is not given. Thanks be to God for the future revelation he has given to mankind through the holy apostles and prophets by his Spirit! There are over 700 quotes or allusions to the Hebrew Bible in the book of Revelation which quotes this verse in part, and gives us the time of this little horn's rule as 42 months (Revelation 13:5). John the revelator describes the final world government as a composition of all the afore-mentioned beasts, who also comes out of the sea (Revelation 13:1-2).

[9] I beheld till the thrones were cast down, and the Ancient of days did sit, whose garment was white as snow, and the hair of his head like the pure wool: his throne was like the fiery flame, and his wheels as burning fire.

The empire of the previously mentioned unified horns or political powers are destroyed by the Ancient of Days (a term for the God of Israel used only in the book of Daniel). The term "cast down" can instead be translated "to be placed or set up" as the NASB translates it. This fits neatly with the parallel account in chapter two where the ten toes are obliterated and replaced by the theocratic future millennial kingdom. These thrones can possibly be the thrones upon which the disciples will sit in the future kingdom (Matthew 20:21), or the thrones sat upon by saints (1 Corinthians 6:2, Revelation 20:4), or maybe both. The Ancient of Day's physical description is parallel to the risen Messiah (Revelation 1:14). ANE thrones were often movable with wheels on the judgment seat and can be related to the concept of a divine chariot.

[10] A fiery stream issued and came forth from before him: thousand thousands ministered unto him, and ten thousand times ten thousand stood before him: the judgment was set, and the books were opened.

The setting is in the throne room of the Ancient of Days with an innumerable host adoring and serving before him, which is similar to the description in the Revelation (Revelation 5:11). The throne of God with fire proceeding from it is also mentioned in the Psalter (Psalm 97:3). The judgment or court proceedings, apparently of the ten horns, is now fixed and the records or official transcripts of all their ungodly deeds which they have committed in ungodliness are brought into evidence.

[11] I beheld then because of the voice of the great words which the horn spake: I beheld even till the beast was slain, and his body destroyed, and given to the burning flame.

Here we have the final confrontation between the beasts or Gentile world powers and the Ancient of Days which corresponds to the Stone suddenly smashing the statue in chapter two. The words of the "little horn" summoned Daniel's attention until its body was destroyed. The state of the body and its burial in the ANE was of the utmost importance. The idea was that their eternal state was reflected upon by the state of their body and a proper burial. The Pharaohs of Egypt would spend their entire life constructing their secure eternal resting place. This is likely why the devil approached the tomb of Moses which was guarded by Michael (Jude 1:9), in order to destroy his body. Even Jezebel, after she was devoured by dogs, was still granted a proper burial by Jehu (2 Kings 9:34). Upon order of the court the little horn's or beast's body is to be destroyed and not given a proper burial, showing the disdained and evil character of the person. Of course, this passage is referenced by the Revelation concerning the destruction of the same person and world system (Revelation 19:20).

[12] As concerning the rest of the beasts, they had their dominion taken away: yet their lives were prolonged for a season and time.

In a flashback, the author comments on the previously mentioned beasts or world powers (Babylon, Medo-Persia, Greece, Rome), that they were somewhat merged into their successors. They were tamed but not destroyed. That is to say, their political, military, etc., methods carried over to a certain degree to the proceeding kingdom. But the fate of the last kingdom, a culmination of all the previous Gentile world powers, the revived future Roman Empire, is total obliteration.

[13] I saw in the night visions, and, behold, one like the Son of man came with the clouds of heaven, and came to the Ancient of days, and they brought him near before him.

The coming of the Son of Man corresponds to the Stone crushing the statue in the parallel dream. The Scriptures often picture the God of Israel as a divine warrior who enters into battle riding on the clouds (Nahum 1:3, Matthew 24:30, Revelation 1:7). In good ANE fashion the divine warrior is formally escorted to the throne by those ministering and surrounding the throne. The term "Son of Man" emphasizes the true and total recognition this person has with mankind. This term was used most frequently by the Lord Jesus of himself (over 30 times), and later in the book is used of Daniel himself (Daniel 8:17). Whereas the second person of the Godhead would rarely appear physically on the stage of history before his incarnation, this term concreted his current membership in humanity. There is great debate as to whether or not God the Father (Ancient of Days) is here symbolically distinguished from God the Son (Son of Man).

[14] And there was given him dominion, and glory, and a kingdom, that all people, nations, and languages, should serve him: his dominion is an everlasting dominion, which shall not pass away, and his kingdom that which shall not be destroyed.

The Ancient of Days here bestows upon the Son of Man the heathen for his inheritance and the uttermost parts of the earth for his possession (Psalm 2:8). A command is given that all the inhabitants of the earth are to worship the Son of Man upon his birthright to rule this kingdom (Psalm 2:12). Unlike the temporary Gentile world powers, the kingdom of the Son of Man is eternal.

[15] I Daniel was grieved in my spirit in the midst of my body, and the visions of my head troubled me.

Upon receiving this revelation, the prophet was profoundly affected or literally pained or sorrowed (*kara*) within himself. Similar reactions happened to Jeremiah and Ezekiel (Jeremiah 4:19, Ezekiel 3:15).

[16] I came near unto one of them that stood by, and asked him the truth of all this. So he told me, and made me know the interpretation of the things.

The prophet now approaches one whom stood by the throne and had witnessed the Ancient of Days bestowing the coming kingdom on the Son of Man and inquires for wisdom in the correct understanding or interpretation of what just happened. Daniel's request is granted and further revelation will now be disclosed to him by the angel.

[17] These great beasts, which are four, are four kings, which shall arise out of the earth.

The fact that the beasts come from the earth (and sometimes the sea) emphasizes the human character or the four world powers which contrasts them with the Son of Man whose character is divine and comes from heaven. The imagery of a beast or Gentile world power arising out of the earth is also mentioned in the Revelation (Revelation 13:11).

[18] But the saints of the most High shall take the kingdom, and possess the kingdom for ever, even for ever and ever.

Those who are holy or set apart to the Most High God will receive (*qebal*) not "take" the kingdom when the Lord comes to establish his dominion (Zechariah 14:5, Jude 1:14-15, Revelation 19:14).

[19] Then I would know the truth of the fourth beast, which was diverse from all the others, exceeding dreadful, whose teeth were of iron, and his nails of brass; which devoured, brake in pieces, and stamped the residue with his feet;

Daniel next inquires to gain certainty about the understanding of the fourth and final empire whose description is previously interpreted by the author (Daniel 7:7). The only new information revealed is that the fourth beast had "iron claws or nails" which underscore the military ferocity of the Roman Empire.

[20] And of the ten horns that were in his head, and of the other which came up, and before whom three fell; even of that horn that had eyes, and a mouth that spake very great things, whose look was more stout than his fellows.

Like the previous verse the exact same description is previously given (Daniel 7:8). The only new element revealed is that, ironically, the little horn's look was greater (*rab*) or larger in appearance than the other horns or ten kings.

[21] I beheld, and the same horn made war with the saints, and prevailed against them;

That is to say, despite his original appearance as small on the political scene, he quickly rises through the ranks to becoming the dominating ruler of the fourth and final empire, crushing all his adversaries.

[22] Until the Ancient of days came, and judgment was given to the saints of the most High; and the time came that the saints possessed the kingdom.

The book of Revelation references the previous verse (Revelation 13:7) and pinpoints these events as taking place 42 months before the Ancient of Days or the Son of Man comes to inherit his rightful kingdom. There is an obvious unification (*'echad)* of the persons of the Ancient of Days and the Son of Man.

[23] Thus he said, The fourth beast shall be the fourth kingdom upon earth, which shall be diverse from all kingdoms, and shall devour the whole earth, and shall tread it down, and break it in pieces.

This is the first direct reference to the fact that the beasts represent world empires. There is another link between the parallel dream in chapter two, as both of the fourth installments of Gentile world powers are called "the fourth kingdom." The fourth kingdom is distinguished from all others as being altered or different for the worse, likely because it is the only kingdom that eats the earth to pieces. Indeed, unless those days were shortened no flesh would survive (Matthew 24:22).

[24] And the ten horns out of this kingdom are ten kings that shall arise: and another shall rise after them; and he shall be diverse from the first, and he shall subdue three kings.

The ten power persons who arise out of the revived Roman Empire shall suddenly be confronted with a previously undisclosed leader that shall take an active part in humbling (*shephal*) three of the ten world leaders. The only new data from the previous mention of the little horn (Daniel 7:8) is that he will arise after the ten kings have been established on the world political scene. These are the same ten kings mentioned in the Revelation (Revelation 17:12).

[25] And he shall speak great words against the most High, and shall wear out the saints of the most High, and think to change times and laws: and they shall be given into his hand until a time and times and the dividing of time.

After the removal of three of the little horn's ten political allies, and unrelenting persecution of those who are set apart to the Son of Man the little horn will first speak great words not "against" but "at the side of" the Most High. That is to say, he will elevate himself as equal to the Most High. This is what Paul is referring to when he mentions the Son of Perdition "sitting in the Temple of God, showing himself that he is God" (2 Thessalonians 2:4). Simultaneously the little horn will prevail in altering the Jewish religious calendar regulated by the law (*torah*) for 42 months (Revelation 12:14). "Times" or set times are mentioned in the Hebrew Bible to denote important events in the Hebrew religious calendar (Ezra 10:14, Nehemiah 10:34).

[26] But the judgment shall sit, and they shall take away his dominion, to consume and to destroy it unto the end.

The verdict that the court in the presence of the Most High has determined concerning the little horn shall "sit" or dwell in judgment and shall condemn his body to the burning flame (Revelation 19:20). The methodical destruction by the Stone as it smashes the statue parallels the destruction of the little horn and the last empire he rules.

[27] And the kingdom and dominion, and the greatness of the kingdom under the whole heaven, shall be given to the people of the saints of the most High, whose kingdom is an everlasting kingdom, and all dominions shall serve and obey him.

After the last beast is destroyed the universal kingdom of the Ancient of Days shall be given to those who have survived or "have not been worn out" by the little horn to administer and enjoy. Furthermore, those in the kingdom of God will minister for and hear/obey their leader designated only as "him." The "him" mentioned here can be none other than the previously mentioned Son of Man who has been given the kingdom by the Ancient of Days (Daniel 7:13-14).

[28] Hitherto is the end of the matter. As for me Daniel, my cogitations much troubled me, and my countenance changed in me: but I kept the matter in my heart.

The beginning and end of the Aramaic section (chapters 2-7), the *lingua franca* of the day, begin and end with two different perspectives of the four great Gentile world powers to rule earth until the coming of the Stone or Son of Man. Though the vision ceased, Daniel's thoughts troubled him so much so that he decided, like Mary, to keep these things about the coming of the Son of Man in his heart (Luke 2:19). But there came a point where Daniel was moved to write the vision, like Mary was later ready to tell Dr. Luke her experience by the visitation of Gabriel.

Daniel 8

[1] In the third year of the reign of king Belshazzar a vision appeared unto me, even unto me Daniel, after that which appeared unto me at the first.

The original autograph and the earliest copies of the book of Daniel have the rest of the book of Daniel composed in Hebrew with the people of Israel primarily in perspective as an audience. The chronological peg in the opening verse dates the vision to 551 BC in the third year of Belshazzar's reign, as the last king of Babylon and crown prince under the auspice of his father King Nabonidus. The reference to the vision "which appeared unto me at the first" is referencing the vision which took place two years earlier in the previous chapter and ties the visions together as sharing the same significance.

[2] And I saw in a vision; and it came to pass, when I saw, that I was at Shushan in the palace, which is in the province of Elam; and I saw in a vision, and I was by the river of Ulai.

The vision begins with Daniel being transported from his home 350 miles away in the city of Babylon to the capital city and palace of the rival Medo-Persian Empire (modern day Iran) near the river Ulai (meaning "mighty") a river which empties itself into the Tigris and Euphrates after their junction, the modern-day name of the river is the Kerah (Herodotus 5:49). The prophet Ezekiel experienced something similar as he was transported from Babylon to the Temple in Jerusalem (Ezekiel 8:3). The region of Elam is an ancient place name with Biblical roots back to Chedorlaomer, King of Elam during the life of Abraham (Genesis 14:1), which lay between Babylon and Persia. The capital city of Shushan was excavated by British archaeologists in the 19th century, most notably by Henry Rawlinson and A.H. Layard but their results were apparently thinly published. Nevertheless, there is still ample evidence for the identity of Shushan. A tablet discovered in Nineveh in 1854 by Layard from the reign of Ashurbanipal the Assyrian ruler in the 7th century BC mentions the city by name and depicts him destroying and punishing the city for their rebellion, destroying the temple of Elam, and sowing their land with salt. The site was rebuilt 100 years or so later by Darius I. Biblically the city is notorious for being the homes of Nehemiah (1:1) and Esther (1:2). Susa is also mentioned in the extra Biblical book Jubilees as belonging to the inheritance of Shem and his descendents (8:21, 9:2). A long-standing legend claims that Shushan is the location of Daniel's retirement and the tomb of the prophet. The site is mentioned by numerous explorers including the 12th century Jewish traveler Benjamin of Tudela. Not surprisingly, William Ouseley the 19th century English author, claims in his work *Walpole's Memoires of the East* that the tomb dates to the Islamic period.

[3] Then I lifted up mine eyes, and saw, and, behold, there stood before the river a ram which had two horns: and the two horns were high; but one was higher than the other, and the higher came up last.

There are many parallels between the writings and experiences of Daniel and Ezekiel. Both of them had their visions in captivity (Daniel 8:2, Ezekiel 1:3), near water (Daniel 8:3, Ezekiel 1:1), were transported in the Spirit (Daniel 8:2, Ezekiel 8:3), had angels appear to them (Daniel 8:15, Ezekiel 40:3), were referred to as son of man (Daniel 8:17, Ezekiel 40:4), and both of their revelations culminate with an emphasis on the Temple in Jerusalem (Daniel 8:13, Ezekiel 40-48). The ram appears on the bank of the river with one horn or source of power exalted above the other horn. This should remind the reader of the two arms of silver (Daniel 2:32) and the lopsided bear (Daniel 7:5). Though the ram has not yet been identified by the prophet or an angel, there is a hint. In symbolism, the original audience would clearly understand that the image of a ram was understood to be and officially used as a symbol of the Persian Empire. Persian coins often depicted a ram's head on one side and a ram at rest on the other.

[4] I saw the ram pushing westward, and northward, and southward; so that no beasts might stand before him, neither was there any that could deliver out of his hand; but he did according to his will, and became great.

The kingdom of the ram gored (*nagach*) his opponents and expanded his kingdom in all directions but eastward because that is the direction from which his kingdom originally pushed. The ram is described as having an unstoppable army and history attests to Cyrus the Great expanding his kingdom in such a fashion. He conquered Asia Minor and Greece to the west, the Medes to the north, and Babylonia, Egypt, etc. to the south "at his will" therefore becoming "great" and establishing the greatest known empire up until his time.

[5] And as I was considering, behold, an he goat came from the west on the face of the whole earth, and touched not the ground: and the goat had a notable horn between his eyes.

As Daniel was discerning (*biyn*) and trying to understand the ram and his movements a he goat came from the western corner of the earth whose military is described as "not touching the ground," that is to say, the speed with which his military moved was unparalleled. The goat's speed should remind us of the previous and connected vision which depicted the leopard as having four wings. The goat originated from the opposite realm of the ram and is depicted as being governed by a conspicuous power person who is oddly enough characterized as having only one highly visible horn compared to the two sources of power represented on the ram. Though the goat, like the ram, has not yet been identified, there is a clue. In regards to imagery the ancient reader would understand the image of a goat was understood to be and officially used as a symbol of the Greek Empire. Greek coins often depicted the symbol of a goat.

[6] And he came to the ram that had two horns, which I had there seen standing before the river, and ran unto him in the fury of his power.

After traveling a long distance from the west, the goat confronts the two horned ram in the heat of his anger on the ram's home territory in the east.

[7] And I saw him come close unto the ram, and he was moved with choler against him, and smote the ram, and brake his two horns: and there was no power in the ram to stand before him, but he cast him down to the ground, and stamped upon him: and there was none that could deliver the ram out of his hand.

The goat, being enraged at the ram, attacked him with force, removed his two sources of power, and none of the allies of the ram could save him from destruction. Though the goat has not been identified the reader is suspicious that it is none other than Alexander the Great and the Greek Empire. The conquests of Alexander over the Medo-Persian Empire began in 334 BC in Hellespont and after conquering Asia Minor destroyed Darius III at the Battle of Issus in 333 BC, after which he took Tyre in a seventh month siege of their island fortress, in 332 BC took Egypt without a battle, in 330 BC conquered Babylon and Shushan, and finally in the Battle of Jhelum in 326 BC conquered the whole known world in a blitzkrieg style never seen before in world history.

[8] Therefore the he goat waxed very great: and when he was strong, the great horn was broken; and for it came up four notable ones toward the four winds of heaven.

At the zenith of the power of the goat his power was suddenly and instantaneously taken away. If indeed this is Alexander the Great this would refer to his untimely and mysterious death at the age of 32 in the former palace of Nebuchadnezzar at Babylon. His body was placed in a gold sarcophagus filled with honey and placed within yet another gold casket and eventually made its way to Alexandria, Egypt. The one horn was replaced by four horns that dispersed to the four corners of the earth. The verse is parallel to the previous vision of the leopard that had four wings (Daniel 7:6).

[9] And out of one of them came forth a little horn, which waxed exceeding great, toward the south, and toward the east, and toward the pleasant land.

A relatively unknown power person would start small but come out of one of the four-fold divisions of the (Greek) empire who, like the previously mentioned little horn in the preceding vision, would surprisingly wax great on the world scene. This cannot be the same power person as this horn emerges from the empire of the goat whereas the little horn mentioned in chapter seven ascends from the revived Roman Empire. Great attention is given to this power person coming from the north, having already possession of the west, and conquering the south, east, and the "pleasant land," which, though enigmatic, can mean none other than Israel (Psalm 106:24).

[10] And it waxed great, even to the host of heaven; and it cast down some of the host and of the stars to the ground, and stamped upon them.

The little horn proverbially grew in size from an unknown power person to being as strong as the armies of heaven. Another reading may be that he, like those who built the Tower of Babel, was aspiring to proverbially reach the heavens where God dwells. At the apex of his power and military might he will cast down religious leaders (stars are used in Revelation 2-3 as to represent religious leaders) from the pleasant land to the ground. That is to say, the little horn will depose the traditional religious Jewish thought and practices in Israel by the removal of the priesthood and religious hierarchy through violence.

[11] Yea, he magnified himself even to the prince of the host, and by him the daily sacrifice was taken away, and the place of his sanctuary was cast down.

The little horn from the empire of the goat, like the little horn from the empire of the revived Roman Empire, will speak blasphemous words and consider himself as God. The Jewish sacrificial system and the Temple itself will be "cast down." This little horn or power person is none other than the infamous 2ⁿᵈ century BC leader Antiochus Epiphanes IV who came out of the horn of the Seleucid dynasty. The inter-testament book 1 Maccabees, likely written in the 2ⁿᵈ century BC some 400 years after the book of Daniel, informs us of how this prophecy was actually fulfilled. It states that Antiochus "sent letters to Jerusalem to profane Sabbath and feasts, to defile the sanctuary and the priests, to build altars and sacred precincts and shrines to idols, to sacrifice swine and unclean animals" (1 Maccabees 1:41-49). Even though Antiochus did not raze the temple like Nebuchadnezzar, he so defiled the Temple in Jerusalem that once the Maccabees regained control of Jerusalem they "rebuilt the sanctuary and the interior of the temple and replaced the altar of burnt offerings" (1 Maccabees 4:43-48).

[12] And an host was given him against the daily sacrifice by reason of transgression, and it cast down the truth to the ground; and it practised, and prospered.

The sins previously mentioned committed by the little horn will empower him to subjugate the people of Israel, put an end to the sacrificial system, and to debase the truth of God's Word. Once again 1 Maccabees informs us that "the books of the torah which they found they tore in pieces and burned with fire…where the book of the covenant was found in the possession of anyone, or if anyone adhered to the torah, the decree of the king (Antiochus) condemned them to death" (1 Maccabees 1:56-57).

[13] Then I heard one saint speaking, and another saint said unto that certain saint which spake, How long shall be the vision concerning the daily sacrifice, and the transgression of desolation, to give both the sanctuary and the host to be trodden under foot?

At the bank of the river Ulai, Daniel observes one angel inquiring from another angel how long the Jewish people, their sacrificial system, their unfettered adherence to the Torah, and the Temple itself will be defiled and persecuted by the little horn (Antiochus).

[14] And he said unto me, Unto two thousand and three hundred days; then shall the sanctuary be cleansed.

Whereas the previously mentioned little horn of the Roman Empire is given 42 months to foam out his own shame, so the little horn from this empire is given exactly 2300 days to do the same. 1 Maccabees informs us that the holy place was properly restored or cleansed in the winter of 164 BC in the Gregorian calendar (1 Maccabees 4:52-59) which gave birth to the Jewish holiday Hanukkah (John 10:22). Working backwards 2300 days from the winter of 164 BC date we can pinpoint the defilement of the Jerusalem Temple by the little horn to 170 BC in the autumn/winter.

[15] And it came to pass, when I, even I Daniel, had seen the vision, and sought for the meaning, then, behold, there stood before me as the appearance of a man.

After the vision had ceased and the prophet had searched to discern the message, a celestial being appeared to him on the banks of the river.

[16] And I heard a man's voice between the banks of Ulai, which called, and said, Gabriel, make this man to understand the vision.

From above the river the prophet heard a supernatural voice commanding the man who stood before him, now identified as Gabriel, to exegete the vision for him. The angel Gabriel is only mentioned in the Hebrew Bible in the book of Daniel but is also mentioned in the book of Luke (Luke 1:19, 26). His name means "man of God" or "warrior of God" and is one of only three angels (the others being Michael and Lucifer) recognized by their proper name in the Scriptures.

[17] So he came near where I stood: and when he came, I was afraid, and fell upon my face: but he said unto me, Understand, O son of man: for at the time of the end shall be the vision.

When he approached Daniel, he, like others in a similar situation, fell to the ground with their face buried in the earth when encountering an angelic being (Revelation 19:10), which was also a customary position when desiring to show respect (1 Samuel 25:23). Gabriel reveals to the prophet the fact that the prophecy is to occur at the end of time. Since it is apparent that the previously mentioned little horn in this chapter is Antiochus Epiphanes IV who reigned in the 2nd century BC, how can the previously mentioned prophecy relate to the end of time, since history tells us that the Greek kingdom continued for another 100 years after Antiochus and the Roman Empire followed? One reading is that verses 1-14 relate to events preceding the first coming of the Messiah and verses 17-26 relate to end of the world events built upon the foundation of the type of little horn (Antiochus) mentioned in verses 1-14 which reach further into Israel's history. Others suggest that "the time of the end" refers to the termination of the little horn and the Greek Empire.

[18] Now as he was speaking with me, I was in a deep sleep on my face toward the ground: but he touched me, and set me upright.

Oftentimes in the Scriptures when a "deep sleep" falls upon a saint, a great gift or message from God is bestowed upon them. After a deep sleep fell upon Adam, Eve was brought to him in a wedding procession (Genesis 2:21), and after a deep sleep fell upon Abram he was informed that his descendents would spend 400 years in bondage (Genesis 15:12) and also told the dimensions of the land promised to him and his descendents. After Daniel slept he was strengthened by the hand of the angel.

[19] And he said, Behold, I will make thee know what shall be in the last end of the indignation: for at the time appointed the end shall be.

Daniel, who understood the vision dimly, is now comforted by Gabriel who informs him that he will finally tell him and the anxious reader about the "appointed time" and how it relates to the nation of Israel.

[20] The ram which thou sawest having two horns are the kings of Media and Persia.

Finally, the reader's suspicions are confirmed as the two-horned ram is identified with the two arms of silver and the lopsided bear; the Medo-Persian Empire. The higher horn which came up last is none other than Cyrus the Great and the other or subservient horn is Darius or Gubaru.

[21] And the rough goat is the king of Grecia: and the great horn that is between his eyes is the first king.

The goat is identified as the Greek Empire and the great horn is Alexander the Great (356-323 BC) the first and primary king of the world-wide Greek Empire.

[22] Now that being broken, whereas four stood up for it, four kingdoms shall stand up out of the nation, but not in his power.

Upon the death of Alexander his kingdom was retooled into four entities. The four kingdoms or horns were Casander who ruled over Greece and Macedonia, Lysimachus who ruled over Thrace and Asia Minor, Antigonus (later Seleueus) who ruled over Babylon, India, Syria, etc. and Ptolemy who ruled over Egypt, Israel and Arabia. Attention is given to the fact that the unified Greek Empire will become weakened or not have the same power upon the death of Alexander.

[23] And in the latter time of their kingdom, when the transgressors are come to the full, a king of fierce countenance, and understanding dark sentences, shall stand up.

Towards the end of the reign of the Greek Empire, when the rebel's iniquity has been completed, that is to say, when their kingdom has run its course, a king negatively portrayed as being skilled in intrigue or able to understand riddles will rise on the geopolitical scene. God is portrayed as allowing the sin of their kingdom to reach an unspeakable measure before he judges them, similar to that of the Amorites (Genesis 15:16). Since the king arises from the previously mentioned Greek kingdom this has to be none other than Antiochus Epiphanes IV.

[24] And his power shall be mighty, but not by his own power: and he shall destroy wonderfully, and shall prosper, and practise, and shall destroy the mighty and the holy people.

The little horn (Antiochus) is characterized as apparently having supernatural power. This anti-Semitic power will enable him to destroy the Jewish people in such an unspeakable way that surpassed and distinguished him from all kings before him. The inter-testament book 2 Maccabees informs us of how this was fulfilled: "He (Antiochus) became as furious as a wild animal, left Egypt and took Jerusalem by storm. Giving his men orders to cut down without mercy everyone they met and to slaughter anyone they found hiding in the houses. They murdered everyone, men and women, boys and girls; even babies were butchered. Three days later Jerusalem had lost 80,000 people: 40,000 killed in the attack and at least that many taken away to be sold as slaves" (2 Maccabees 5:11-14).

[25] And through his policy also he shall cause craft to prosper in his hand; and he shall magnify himself in his heart, and by peace shall destroy many: he shall also stand up against the Prince of princes; but he shall be broken without hand.

Through the evil insight of Antiochus treachery against the Jewish people shall rush to success. He magnified himself in his heart by proclaiming his subjects to worship him as the incarnation of the Greek God Zeus and thereby took the title "Theos Epiphanes" meaning something like "the manifestation of God." He was the first Greek king to proclaim himself as God on coins, where he was portrayed as Zeus on the throne with the inscription "King Antiochus, God manifest, Bearing Victory." Thinking himself to be God, Antiochus, like Herod Agrippa 1 (Acts 12:23) was killed "without hand" or in a supernatural fashion similar to the stone that was cut out of the mountain without hands (Daniel 2:45). 1 Maccabees records the death of Antiochus IV (1 Maccabees 6:1-16) who interestingly associates the demise of his health with the looting of the Temple in Jerusalem and the destruction of the Jewish people.

[26] And the vision of the evening and the morning which was told is true: wherefore shut thou up the vision; for it shall be for many days.

Gabriel concludes his interpretation and exegesis of the vision to the prophet and instructed him to seal up the written document upon which this prophecy would be written in order to preserve it because it is designated for the distant future.

[27] And I Daniel fainted, and was sick certain days; afterward I rose up, and did the king's business; and I was astonished at the vision, but none understood it.

Afterwards the prophet was exhausted and grieved but upon recuperation continued his ministry in the Babylonian Empire under the rule of Belshazzar. Daniel, being stupefied by the vision, apparently shared it with others in his circle but no one could entirely understand the full meaning of the vision.

Daniel 9

[1] In the first year of Darius the son of Ahasuerus, of the seed of the Medes, which was made king over the realm of the Chaldeans;

The chronological peg given in verse one dates the events of the chapter to around 538 BC, shortly after the Babylonian Empire under the rule of the crown prince Belshazzar was covertly conquered by the Medo-Persian Empire under the command of Darius. This Darius is known in extra biblical sources as Gubaru and is here given a brief genealogy. His father Ahasuerus is not the same Ahasuerus or Xerxes I mentioned in the books of Ezra and Esther. Ahasuerus (meaning "I will be poor and silent") is the Hebrew form of the name or title of the king of Persia, Xerxes. Darius was made king over the region of Babylon by Cyrus the Great, the Median Empire being the lesser power (recalling the lopsided bear) and subservient to the Persian Empire.

[2] In the first year of his reign I Daniel understood by books the number of the years, whereof the word of the LORD came to Jeremiah the prophet, that he would accomplish seventy years in the desolations of Jerusalem.

At the very beginning of the Medo-Persian Empire Daniel studied the scrolls of Jeremiah (25:11-12, 29:10-19) likely brought with him from Jerusalem, written some 65 years earlier, to determine where the Jewish people stood in the timetable of their dispersion for their sinful idolatry and willful neglect of the appointed sabbatical years (Leviticus 26:32-35) and waiting for God to turn away their captivity and bring them again to the place where he caused them to be carried away. Daniel was inquiring of YHWH what method he would use to bring this to fulfillment and the exact day it would happen (Ezra 1).

[3] And I set my face unto the Lord God, to seek by prayer and supplication, with fasting, and sackcloth, and ashes:

Daniel gives or sets his attention to the Lord God (Adonai Elohim), a compound name of the Most High, by putting aside all of his normal daily routines so he can devote all his time to pray, fast, and privately dress in sackcloth and ashes, an outward expression of an inwardly broken heart. Sackcloth and ashes likely consisted of a rough and coarse animal hair garment while cold ashes were placed on the head. Some have suggested that Daniel offered this prayer on the Day of Atonement, but the descriptions of what the Jews were to do on the Yom Kippur do not specifically mention fasting or dressing in sackcloth and ashes but only that the Jews were "to afflict their souls" (Leviticus 16:29-31). Nevertheless, this chapter is recognized along with Ezra 9 and Nehemiah 9 as being one of the greatest prayers in the Hebrew Bible.

[4] And I prayed unto the LORD my God, and made my confession, and said, O Lord, the great and dreadful God, keeping the covenant and mercy to them that love him, and to them that keep his commandments;

Daniel directs his prayer to YHWH, the first time the divine name is used in the book is in chapter nine. Outside of the Gentile world system and influences and now in the quietness of his own heart the prophet can beseech the covenant making God of Israel, YHWH. The covenants referred to here are no doubt the Abrahamic and Mosaic covenants and all the promises, blessings, and curses they entail. The name YHWH has been found on approximately 50 archeological objects with around half of them being discovered from deep in the modern day Negev at a site called Kuntillet Ajrud.

[5] We have sinned, and have committed iniquity, and have done wickedly, and have rebelled, even by departing from thy precepts and from thy judgments:

As the Jews who were in exile were supposed to do, the prophet confesses his iniquity to God (Leviticus 26:40). The prophet includes himself (we) as being part and parcel of the chosen nation who has rebelled against their God by turning away from His Torah (instruction) and turning unto false gods. This is an accumulation of sins that started long before Daniel and encompassed all the crimes of all the kings of Judah and their subjects and culminated with the destruction of the Temple by Nebuchadnezzar in 586 BC and their dispersion from Israel. The majority of this prayer is confessional and praise-giving in nature.

[6] Neither have we hearkened unto thy servants the prophets, which spake in thy name to our kings, our princes, and our fathers, and to all the people of the land.

The people and hierarchy of Judah were notorious for not hearkening to and even slaying their own prophets. Jeremiah was cast into the sewer pit (Jeremiah 38:1-6), Isaiah was according to tradition sawn asunder (Hebrews 11:37), and the Lord Jesus mentioned how the first century Jew's ancestors killed their own prophets (Luke 11:46).

[7] O Lord, righteousness belongeth unto thee, but unto us confusion of faces, as at this day; to the men of Judah, and to the inhabitants of Jerusalem, and unto all Israel, that are near, and that are far off, through all the countries whither thou hast driven them, because of their trespass that they have trespassed against thee.

The prophet characterizes the chosen nation as having a face of shame because of their unfaithfulness towards the God of Israel. Shame in the ANE was a stigma that we can hardly understand in our modern day 21st century. In a slow paced, conservative, tight knit world like ancient Israel, an offense committed against a person or God for that matter would result in losing one of your greatest and most respected qualities; honor, thereby losing the ability to establish credibility.

[8] O Lord, to us belongeth confusion of face, to our kings, to our princes, and to our fathers, because we have sinned against thee.

Daniel characterizes all of Israel as transgressing against the Lord and as having a face covered with shame, whether them, their ancestors, their kings, those in dispersion in Babylon, Egypt, or the pitiful remnant left in Israel to work the land and provide for the needs of the Babylonian Empire. God has not failed his people, they have failed him.

[9] To the Lord our God belong mercies and forgivenesses, though we have rebelled against him;

Though the people of Israel have moved with sedition against their God, he is characterized as being gracious, merciful, slow to anger and of great kindness (Exodus 34:6-7, Deuteronomy 4:31, Psalm 86:15, Jonah 4:2).

[10] Neither have we obeyed the voice of the LORD our God, to walk in his laws, which he set before us by his servants the prophets.

Daniel is echoing the voice of Moses, who similarly stated "as the nations which the LORD destroyed before your face, so shall ye perish; because ye would not be obedient unto the voice of the LORD your God" (Deuteronomy 8:20). Just like their father Adam who heard the voice of the LORD his God and disobeyed the clear instruction of YHWH the people of Israel too learned the hard way that obedience is the key to blessing.

[11] Yea, all Israel have transgressed thy law, even by departing, that they might not obey thy voice; therefore the curse is poured upon us, and the oath that is written in the law of Moses the servant of God, because we have sinned against him.

The Torah or instruction the people have transgressed is obviously the Mosaic Law, but more specifically the curse being poured upon the nation comes from the so-called blessings and curses chapter of Deuteronomy 28. The conditions of the blessings in the land promise the nation of Israel an abundance of family oriented and agriculturally based oaths and also to be set on high above all nations of the earth, but if the nation does not observe the Torah, destruction and dispersion - like the Babylonian exile - are promised. What a far cry from the same nation who, after receiving the Torah, said "All the words which the LORD hath said will we do" (Exodus 24:3).

[12] And he hath confirmed his words, which he spake against us, and against our judges that judged us, by bringing upon us a great evil: for under the whole heaven hath not been done as hath been done upon Jerusalem.

God is not a man that he should lie (Numbers 23:19). Every jot and tittle promised in the book of Moses, whether a blessing or curse, has come to pass for the nation of Israel. The destruction of the Temple of Solomon and Jerusalem by Nebuchadnezzar in his 30-month siege was so horrendous that the inhabitants were brought to cannibalism, starvation, and other lewd behaviors of total depravity (Lamentation 4-5). This was the culmination of the warnings of the prophets Isaiah, Micah, Jeremiah and Ezekiel. As far as we know no other city under the sun had suffered such a catastrophic end as the City of the Great King, Jerusalem (Ezekiel 24:16-27).

[13] As it is written in the law of Moses, all this evil is come upon us: yet made we not our prayer before the LORD our God, that we might turn from our iniquities, and understand thy truth.

Among other purposes, the Torah was given to govern the nation of Israel as a theocratic kingdom while Israel had a king. It functioned almost as a constitution, a covenant that was written and therefore unchangeable and of a binding character. Nevertheless, the nation slowly but surely did not give their attention to the written Word. Oftentimes in Scripture examples are given that the more light a nation is given by the God of Israel (Nineveh, Israel, etc.) the more responsible the nation is to that light, and the sooner they turn away from that light the more apt they are to be totally destroyed.

[14] Therefore hath the LORD watched upon the evil, and brought it upon us: for the LORD our God is righteous in all his works which he doeth: for we obeyed not his voice.

The eyes of the LORD thy God are always upon it (Deuteronomy 11:12), that is to say, always upon Israel, and he has watched the unpleasant behavior of his chosen people and chastised them with the destruction of their city and the Babylonian dispersion which they so fittingly deserved. God is characterized by the prophet as being reliable and consistent in everything he says and does.

[15] And now, O Lord our God, that hast brought thy people forth out of the land of Egypt with a mighty hand, and hast gotten thee renown, as at this day; we have sinned, we have done wickedly.

Daniel references God as the saving God who miraculously delivered his people out of Egypt and the report of his wonders melted the hearts of the people of Canaan. The prophet, like the Psalmist, begs for a return to the land even though the people did not keep the Torah by stating "we have sinned with our fathers, we have committed iniquity, we have done wickedly" (Psalm 106:6).

[16] O Lord, according to all thy righteousness, I beseech thee, let thine anger and thy fury be turned away from thy city Jerusalem, thy holy mountain: because for our sins, and for the iniquities of our fathers, Jerusalem and thy people are become a reproach to all that are about us.

In this prayer of Daniel, which is rooted or based in confession and praise to YHWH, this is the only petition to the Lord. The prophet's request is to restore the Jewish people to their homeland and the capital city of Jerusalem by fulfilling his promise that the captivity in Babylon would only last 70 years. The Jews directed their prayers like many other cultures in the ANE to an elevated location which was also the abode of their deity. The Tower of Babel, whose top may reach unto heaven, the "high places" in Israel during the monarchy, and even Mt. Hermon or Mt. Seir were all elevated places where the peoples went up to worship their god.

[17] Now therefore, O our God, hear the prayer of thy servant, and his supplications, and cause thy face to shine upon thy sanctuary that is desolate, for the Lord's sake.

Daniel now zeroes in on the desolate Temple Mount on Mt. Zion with his petition to beseech God to cause his presence to shine (*'owr*) upon, or in other words, to rebuild his Temple in Jerusalem - as Daniel understood the 70-year captivity to culminate shortly for the sake of God's reputation. Daniel is likely referring to the post-Solomonic Psalm 80 which is the only other portion in the Hebrew Bible which appeals to God to cause his "face to shine" upon his people because the LORD GOD of hosts is angry with his people Israel.

[18] O my God, incline thine ear, and hear; open thine eyes, and behold our desolations, and the city which is called by thy name: for we do not present our supplications before thee for our righteousnesses, but for thy great mercies.

In the great prayer of King Hezekiah upon the impending invasion of the Assyrian war machine, the prophet Daniel echoes the same words as the king; "incline thine ear, O LORD, and hear, open thine eyes" (Isaiah 37:17). Both the king and the prophet could be calling up from memory the Psalm of David (17:6), the only other time that phrase is used. The purpose of the petition is to rebuild the ruins of the Temple and Jerusalem so the people can once again approach their God in his Temple.

[19] O Lord, hear; O Lord, forgive; O Lord, hearken and do; defer not, for thine own sake, O my God: for thy city and thy people are called by thy name.

As Daniel concludes his prayer the prophet's main concern is that the honor of the God of Israel would not be shamed. Therefore, he begs God to cause the mountain of his holiness, the joy of the whole earth, to be rebuilt and not delayed for, among other reasons, to cause the Gentile nations to cease from saying "where is their God"?

[20] And whiles I was speaking, and praying, and confessing my sin and the sin of my people Israel, and presenting my supplication before the LORD my God for the holy mountain of my God;

It is significant that Daniel was verbally petitioning the Lord with prayer. In the world of the Bible power was perceived to be contained in the spoken word. God created the world by his speech (Psalm 33:6-9), Balaam could only speak the word that God put into his mouth (Numbers 22:35), in the beginning was the Word (John 1:1), faith comes by hearing (Romans 10:17), we are to take the sword of the Spirit which is the word (*rhema*) of God. Therefore, by speaking aloud the prayer those in the ANE would have understood the petition to be authoritative and binding. Those who perceive this prayer as taking place on The Day of Atonement give attention to the fact that Daniel, like Aaron, interceded for himself and his house (Leviticus 16:6).

[21] Yea, whiles I was speaking in prayer, even the man Gabriel, whom I had seen in the vision at the beginning, being caused to fly swiftly, touched me about the time of the evening oblation.

Before the prophet was done speaking his petition, Gabriel (meaning "warrior of God" or "man of God") approached Daniel at around 3 or 4 PM (1 Kings 18:29), the time of the evening sacrifice in Jerusalem. The translation "being caused to fly swiftly" is difficult to translate but likely inaccurate. A better translation would be "in my great fatigue." Nevertheless, Daniel, still being locked into the set prayer times revolving around the now destroyed Temple refers to the previous encounter he had with Gabriel (Daniel 8:16) some 13 years earlier when he helped the prophet understand the vision that pertained to "the time of the end."

[22] And he informed me, and talked with me, and said, O Daniel, I am now come forth to give thee skill and understanding.

Gabriel's objective is to assist Daniel's understanding about the correct interpretation of the scrolls of Jeremiah he was studying concerning the accomplishment of the 70-year captivity.

[23] At the beginning of thy supplications the commandment came forth, and I am come to shew thee; for thou art greatly beloved: therefore understand the matter, and consider the vision.

As soon as Daniel began his prayer Gabriel was commanded to go, apparently from the third heaven to Daniel's abode for the purpose of making known (*nagad*) to him the correct reading of the prophecy, because of the precious love God and possibly his host had for the prophet. The vision Gabriel wants the prophet to discern is the remaining of the chapter.

[24] Seventy weeks are determined upon thy people and upon thy holy city, to finish the transgression, and to make an end of sins, and to make reconciliation for iniquity, and to bring in everlasting righteousness, and to seal up the vision and prophecy, and to anoint the most Holy.

Gabriel informs Daniel that 70 sevens (*shabuwa*) that is, 70 times seven, are decreed or marked out for the Jewish people, not the church, which was a mystery which had not yet been made known to the sons of men, and their capital city of Jerusalem. "Weeks" or sevens means a unit of seven, seven of anything, and in this context, means years. The purpose of the 490-year period has six goals according to this verse. The first three goals put an end to human rebellion. The second three goals relate to kingdom policies such as establishing "everlasting righteousness" that is to say the Kingdom of God on earth, as well as putting an end to any further need of special revelation, and finally consecrating the most Holy Place which was defiled by the little horn. Gabriel is correcting Daniel's misunderstanding about the kingdom being set up at the end of 70 years and revealing to the prophet the program of God which would bring in that kingdom.

[25] Know therefore and understand, that from the going forth of the commandment to restore and to build Jerusalem unto the Messiah the Prince shall be seven weeks, and threescore and two weeks: the street shall be built again, and the wall, even in troublous times.

The going forth of the command to restore and rebuild the walls of Jerusalem took place in 445 BC during the 20th year of the reign of Artaxerxes I, the king of the Persian Empire (Nehemiah 2:4-8). The proclamation of this decree began the 70x7, but on closer look the verse states that it is 69x7 or a 483-year countdown until the appearance of Messiah the Prince in Jerusalem. The appearance of the Messiah or his public offer of himself as King at the end of 483-year period was the Triumphal Entry (Matthew 21:1-11). If we subtract 483 years from 445 BC, then in approximately 33 A.D., if we use the standard ancient 360-day Jewish calendar, (i.e. 1260 days equals 42 months), that is to say in 173,880 days, the Jewish Messiah will reveal himself in Jerusalem. Yeshua (Jesus) is the Jewish Messiah.

[26] And after threescore and two weeks shall Messiah be cut off, but not for himself: and the people of the prince that shall come shall destroy the city and the sanctuary; and the end thereof shall be with a flood, and unto the end of the war desolations are determined.

Unexpectedly and tragically after the 483rd year (69x7 or 173,880 days) but before the 70th year, that is to say in 33 A.D., the Messiah will die with nothing; meaning the Messiah was slain without honor (crucifixion) and abandoned by his friends. After the death of the Messiah "the people of the prince" not "the prince" shall come and destroy the city and the Temple. The nationality of the people who will destroy Jerusalem and the prince that *shall* come are identical. Of course, history tells us that the Roman Empire destroyed Jerusalem in AD 70 under the direction of Titus, fulfilling this verse. The prince *that shall come* is the "little horn" that comes out of the revived Roman Empire previously mentioned in chapter seven. Since the little horn, beast or antichrist must be of the same nationality as the people who destroyed the Temple (in AD 70) it is this verse that informs us that he will be a gentile of Roman origin.

[27] And he shall confirm the covenant with many for one week: and in the midst of the week he shall cause the sacrifice and the oblation to cease, and for the overspreading of abominations he shall make it desolate, even until the consummation, and that determined shall be poured upon the desolate.

To the reader's surprise there is still one "week" or unit of seven remaining. Scripture and history give us absolutely no evidence of a Roman ruler making a seven-year pact with the nation of Israel. Therefore, there is an unexpected gap between the 69th and 70th year. This is the future "week" or seven-year period mentioned in the book of Revelation. During this gap of almost 2000 years Israel has been "broken off" and the church "being a wild olive tree" (Romans 11:17) has been grafted into the program of God. The church is "the mystery which hath been hid from ages and from generations but *now* is made manifest to his saints" (Colossians 1:26). Not only was this mystery unknown in antiquity, that is to say, on the pages of the Hebrew Bible but even in the recent generation of the original autographs of the New Testament. The church came upon the world suddenly and unexpectedly. Nevertheless, the 70x7 clock has been paused at 69x7 until the *prince that shall come,* that is to say, the little horn or the antichrist confirms a covenant with Israel for a "week." In the middle of the future "week" the little horn shall declare himself God, wear out the saints, and change the Jewish sacrificial system (Daniel 7:25). What does "and for the overspreading of abominations he shall make it desolate" mean? The word overspreading (*kanaph*) means wing or corner and can be translated "an overspreading influence" which likely refers to the pinnacle of the Temple in Jerusalem. This refers to the worship of the little horn or antichrist when he declares himself to be God (2 Thessalonians 2:4). The word abomination can refer to an image, meaning that an image of the little horn or beast will be erected (Revelation 13:15) on the pinnacle of the Temple. Interestingly, Jewish rabbinic tradition states that the Messiah will manifest himself standing on the pinnacle of the Temple (Pesiqta Rabbati 162a). After waiting for millennia, many in the nation of Israel who are alive in the 70th week will be deceived and accept the little horn, the antichrist, as their Messiah. Nevertheless, the true Messiah will come at the end of the 70th week and the nation of Israel will repent "and they shall look upon me whom they have pierced" (Zechariah

12:10), and "that determined shall be poured upon the desolate" that is to say "the Lord will slay with the breath of his mouth and bring to an end (the wicked one) by the appearance of his coming" (2 Thessalonians 2:8). The beast and the false prophet will be thrown into the lake of fire (Revelation 19:20) and the true Messiah, the Lord Jesus Christ will establish his 1000-year kingdom on earth (Revelation 20).

Daniel 10

[1] In the third year of Cyrus king of Persia a thing was revealed unto Daniel, whose name was called Belteshazzar; and the thing was true, but the time appointed was long: and he understood the thing, and had understanding of the vision.

The chronological peg in verse one permits us to date the events in this chapter to 536 BC, that is, three years after the Medo-Persian Empire conquered the Babylonian Empire and approximately two years after the prophecy of the seventy sevens. The date of 536 BC is an important note because this informs us that Zerubbabel (meaning "sown or born in Babel") and Joshua (meaning "salvation") were already in Jerusalem to begin the rebuilding of the walls, the Temple, and the city of Jerusalem. The phrase "the thing was true but the time appointed was long" is probably not the best translation and could be read "the thing (message) was true and concerned great warfare." Unlike the previous revelations when Daniel needed clarification of the correct exegesis which was given to him by Gabriel, this vision "he understood."

[2] In those days I Daniel was mourning three full weeks.

The scene opens up with Daniel lamenting for three "weeks." The Hebrew clarifies these as "weeks of days" in contrast to its previous use in chapter nine.

[3] I ate no pleasant bread, neither came flesh nor wine in my mouth, neither did I anoint myself at all, till three whole weeks were fulfilled.

Since the 21-day period ended on the 24th day of Nisan, the first month of the year, Daniel was semi-fasting during the entire Passover feast. Passover begins on the 14th day of the first month (Exodus 12:6). Likely he was dedicating his time to praying for the current dilemma his kinfolk was now facing in their effort to rebuild Jerusalem.

[4] And in the four and twentieth day of the first month, as I was by the side of the great river, which is Hiddekel;

After his fasting, the prophet appears on the banks of the Tigris River. The only other mention of the river Hiddekel is it being one of the four heads that parted from the river that came out of Eden (Genesis 2:14).

[5] Then I lifted up mine eyes, and looked, and behold a certain man clothed in linen, whose loins were girded with fine gold of Uphaz:

Once again, the prophet is visited on the banks of a river by a celestial being. The man was clothed in linen, white and clean, and upheld with a belt of the finest gold from Uphaz. The place name Uphaz is possibly

Ophir, a region renowned for its natural resources (Job 22:24). If the word Uphaz is not a corruption of the place name Ophir, then it is not a place name but means something like "the finest" gold.

[6] His body also was like the beryl, and his face as the appearance of lightning, and his eyes as lamps of fire, and his arms and his feet like in colour to polished brass, and the voice of his words like the voice of a multitude.

The description of the "certain man" which is yet to be identified parallels the description of the resurrected Lord Jesus Christ (Revelation 1:13-15). Daniel compares the radiance of his body with one of the stones in the High Priests' breastplate. Nevertheless, the identity of this person is still not clear.

[7] And I Daniel alone saw the vision: for the men that were with me saw not the vision; but a great quaking fell upon them, so that they fled to hide themselves.

Daniel, like Paul, later were in a company of men when encountered from on high but neither of the companies of men received the message, only the prophets (Acts 9:7). (It is like in the Saul narrative that the men with him heard the "voice" as a sound but did not hear the "voice" as articulating the three statements to Saul. Similarly, when a voice from heaven came to Jesus (John 12:29) the Greek thinking crowd, being logical in nature, said that it thundered, whereas the Hebrews claimed that an angel spoke).

[8] Therefore I was left alone, and saw this great vision, and there remained no strength in me: for my comeliness was turned in me into corruption, and I retained no strength.

After seeing Daniel turn deathly pale and fall to the ground without strength the company of men with him fled away, likely being aware of the prophet's prior dreadful and awesome experiences of receiving special revelation.

[9] Yet heard I the voice of his words: and when I heard the voice of his words, then was I in a deep sleep on my face, and my face toward the ground.

With his face buried in the earth because of exhaustion and possibly to worship the messenger (Revelation 19:10), the prophet fell into a deep sleep. As mentioned earlier (Daniel 8:18), oftentimes when a "deep sleep" falls upon a saint a great message from God is revealed unto them.

[10] And, behold, an hand touched me, which set me upon my knees and upon the palms of my hands.

Like the resurrected Lord Jesus who "laid his right hand" on the prostrate prophet (Revelation 1:17), so this still unidentified messenger does the same.

[11] And he said unto me, O Daniel, a man greatly beloved, understand the words that I speak unto thee, and stand upright: for unto thee am I now sent. And when he had spoken this word unto me, I stood trembling.

This messenger, like Gabriel who visited the prophet two years earlier (Daniel 9:23), reminds Daniel that he is highly esteemed in the throne room of the Most High God. The "man" who was described in the same manner as the resurrected Lord Jesus proclaims to Daniel that he was "sent". There are over 50 occurrences in the New Testament stating that the Father sent the Son.

[12] Then said he unto me, Fear not, Daniel: for from the first day that thou didst set thine heart to understand, and to chasten thyself before thy God, thy words were heard, and I am come for thy words.

Just as the resurrected Lord Jesus told John "fear not" after he touched him (Revelation 1:17), so the pre-incarnate Lord Jesus does the same to the prophet Daniel. Daniel's experience echoes the testimony of the prophet Isaiah who said "before they call, I will answer; and while they are yet speaking, I will hear." The Lord Jesus was sent as soon as Daniel began his fasting and prayer, "from the first day that thou didst set thine heart to understand" three weeks earlier.

[13] But the prince of the kingdom of Persia withstood me one and twenty days: but, lo, Michael, one of the chief princes, came to help me; and I remained there with the kings of Persia.

The reason he was delayed was because the "prince of the kingdom of Persia," apparently a representative of spiritual wickedness in high places that was designated over the kingdom of Persia took a stand against him. If that wasn't troubling enough, Michael (meaning "who is like Elohim") the archangel was sent to assist the "man" (whom we have surmised is the pre-incarnate Christ) in his battle with the prince of Persia. There were occurrences when the Lord had the assistance of angels in his earthly ministry (Matthew 4:11). And in another place, he said "thinkest thou that I cannot now pray to my Father, and he shall presently give me more than twelve legions of angels" (Matthew 26:53)? Nevertheless he "had remained" or "had been left" with the prince of Persia; this term can carry the concept of a position of superiority such as on a battlefield.

[14] Now I am come to make thee understand what shall befall thy people in the latter days: for yet the vision is for many days.

After the messenger's delay of three weeks he comes to Daniel at the banks of the Tigris River and informs the prophet the he will explain the vision that pertains to the nation of Israel in "the latter days" and that the events thereof are for a time yet to come. The term "latter days" does not necessarily have a narrow definition and does not always pertain to "the end of the world" or eschatological events. An example would be the swan song of Jacob, who tells his sons what "shall befall you in the last days" (Genesis 49:1).

[15] And when he had spoken such words unto me, I set my face toward the ground, and I became dumb.

After hearing the voice which sounded like a tumult the prophet buried his face in the earth, in contrast to "lifting up his eyes" and became dumb (*'alam*) like John, who also later fell at his feet as dead (Revelation 1:17).

[16] And, behold, one like the similitude of the sons of men touched my lips: then I opened my mouth, and spake, and said unto him that stood before me, O my lord, by the vision my sorrows are turned upon me, and I have retained no strength.

Just as the prophet Isaiah needed to be cleansed of his sins before hearing God's latter days timetable for the nation of Israel (Isaiah 6:6-13, "...and he laid it upon my mouth (live coal), and said, Lo, this hath touched thy lips; and thine iniquity is taken away, and thy sin purged...and he said, Go, and tell this people"), so Daniel also now becomes qualified.

[17] For how can the servant of this my lord talk with this my lord? for as for me, straightway there remained no strength in me, neither is there breath left in me.

Sensing an overwhelming feeling of his uncleanness in the presence of the living God, the prophet could hardly breathe and asks the "man" a rhetorical question.

[18] Then there came again and touched me one like the appearance of a man, and he strengthened me,

The messenger who looked like a man caused the prophet to regain his strength and courage by touching the prophet. The Lord Jesus also touched the prophet John with his right hand (Revelation 1:17) to strengthen him. It doesn't say which hand the "man" in this verse used, but like the Lord he likely used his right hand, the "clean hand" in the thought and practice of the ANE. The left hand was used for, among other unclean purposes, to clean yourself and it is always the "right hand" of the Lord that holds his people (Psalm Psalm 73:23) and does valiantly (Psalm 118:16).

[19] And said, O man greatly beloved, fear not: peace be unto thee, be strong, yea, be strong. And when he had spoken unto me, I was strengthened, and said, Let my lord speak; for thou hast strengthened me.

Again, the prophet is reminded that the throne room of God delights in him and his ministry. Daniel, being "broken" from encountering the "man" is told that peace (*shalom*) or more accurately completeness, should be unto him, and he is told twice (for reason of emphasis) to be courageous and firm in the light of the person he is encountering and the revelation he shall receive. Translators will at times avoid repetition by stating "be strong and of a good courage" (Joshua 1:8) even though the phrase could be translated as it is in this verse. Upon regaining his faculties, the prophet is ready to understand.

[20] Then said he, Knowest thou wherefore I come unto thee? and now will I return to fight with the prince of Persia: and when I am gone forth, lo, the prince of Grecia shall come.

The celestial "man" asks the prophet if he is privy as to why he came to the prophet and then without waiting for a response goes on state that he will continue back to where he came from but along the way shall resume battle with his foe. This war with the spiritual wickedness in high places took place in 536 BC and would continue for another 200 years until the termination of the Medo-Persian Empire when the leopard with four wings of a fowl would arise. Finally, he informs Daniel that another principality (the Greek Empire) which obviously follows the Medo-Persian Empire, will continue the war against himself and his host.

[21] But I will shew thee that which is noted in the scripture of truth: and there is none that holdeth with me in these things, but Michael your prince.

The messenger will make known or declare (*nagad*) to the prophet the rest of the prophecy which is noted here as "the scripture of truth." No other angel, not even Gabriel, was apparently qualified to assist the Lord in this level of upcoming warfare except Michael the arch or chief of the angels (Jude 1:9).

Daniel 11

[1] Also I in the first year of Darius the Mede, even I, stood to confirm and to strengthen him.

The reader should avoid the unnecessary chapter division here and continue reading the account with the previous chapter's background information in mind. The chapter and verse divisions were not part of the original autographs or later copies. The "man" ministering to Daniel states that he recently was an encouragement and protector of "Darius the Mede," which likely meant he somehow, in the free decision of the king, assisted him, just as Cyrus made the decree for the Jews to return to their homeland and rebuild their walls, the city, and the Temple (Ezra 1:1). Another reading seems to fit the context better, the Septuagint reads "in the first year of Cyrus" and not Darius the Mede. Cyrus is previously mentioned in the vision (Daniel 10:1) and Darius is not and Cyrus more than Darius would logically need to be strengthened since he was responsible for the decree to send the nation of Israel back home. Nevertheless, either reading does not injure the overall flow of the prophecy.

[2] And now will I shew thee the truth. Behold, there shall stand up yet three kings in Persia; and the fourth shall be far richer than they all: and by his strength through his riches he shall stir up all against the realm of Grecia.

The messenger informs the prophet that three kings will follow Cyrus (550-530 BC). History has shown these kings to be Cambyses (530-522 BC), Smerdis (522 BC), and Darius I Hystaspes (521-486 BC). Special attention is then given to the fourth king of Persia, the infamous Xerxes (Ahasuerus) of the book of Esther. Artaxerxes indeed "stirred up all" against the up-and-coming Greek Empire in a full-fledged war (481-479 BC). According to the Greek historian Herodotus in the *Persian Wars,* this prophecy in Daniel was fulfilled when Xerxes went "…to throw a bridge over the Hellespont and march an army through Europe against Greece."

[3] And a mighty king shall stand up, that shall rule with great dominion, and do according to his will.

In enigmatic fashion Daniel is informed that another unnamed king after the fourth king (Xerxes) will arise on the geopolitical world scene and obtain world dominion as he pleases.

[4] And when he shall stand up, his kingdom shall be broken, and shall be divided toward the four winds of heaven; and not to his posterity, nor according to his dominion which he ruled: for his kingdom shall be plucked up, even for others beside those.

When this mysterious king will be at the height of his power he shall perish and his empire will be weakened by being divided into four portions. Of course, the mysterious king is none other than Alexander the Great and the four wings or four heads (Daniel 7:6) are Casander (Greece), Lysimachus (Asia Minor), Seleueus (Middle East), and Ptolemy (Egypt, Israel, etc.). The prophecy jumps about 150 years into the future after the death of Xerxes and skips the remaining six Persian kings and brings us to the life and death of Alexander the Great and the division of his empire.

[5] And the king of the south shall be strong, and one of his princes; and he shall be strong above him, and have dominion; his dominion shall be a great dominion.

Ptolemy, who ruled the southern section of the Greek Empire, Alexandria, Egypt being his headquarters, will rise in dominion but unexpectedly one of his commanders will exercise and rule with more authority than he. The "prince" in this passage should be identified as the Greek commander Seleucus, the founder of the Seleucid dynasty and the yet to be mentioned "king of the north."

[6] And in the end of years they shall join themselves together; for the king's daughter of the south shall come to the king of the north to make an agreement: but she shall not retain the power of the arm; neither shall he stand, nor his arm: but she shall be given up, and they that brought her, and he that begat her, and he that strengthened her in these times.

The two dynasties will attempt to concrete their alliances through a political marriage, a very common method of diplomacy in the ANE. Solomon had 700 political wives and princes and 300 concubines during his reign (1 Kings 11:1-3). Unbeknown to the reader there is more than a 30-year gap between the events of the previous verse and this verse (280-249 BC). The daughter of the king of the south (Ptolemy Lagus) is identified as Berenice I of Egypt (340-268?), who according to this verse after an indefinite period of time will not retain any power in the northern kingdom, that is to say their marriage will not last, and she and her father will no longer retain the political connections needed between the southern kingdom in Egypt and the northern kingdom which should be identified as Syria.

[7] But out of a branch of her roots shall one stand up in his estate, which shall come with an army, and shall enter into the fortress of the king of the north, and shall deal against them, and shall prevail:

A descendent from the family tree of Berenice shall come up from Egypt to relieve her of her shame and attack the headquarters of the king of the north in Syria and overthrow the Seleucid dynasty. History has shown this branch to be Ptolemy Euergetes (who reigned from 246-222 BC), her brother.

[8] And shall also carry captives into Egypt their gods, with their princes, and with their precious vessels of silver and of gold; and he shall continue more years than the king of the north.

Euergetes marched in parade fashion with the booty taken from Syria through Israel back to his headquarters in Egypt. History reports that Euergetes carried some 2500 idols from Syria to Egypt, many of which were taken from Egypt during the reign of the Persian king Cambyses. After replacing the stolen relics, the common people in Egypt bestowed upon Euergetes the nickname "the benefactor." A prophecy is also given that he will live longer than his counterpart in the north. According to the canon of Ptolemy, Euergetes reigned 25 years (246-222 BC) and lived three/four years longer than Seleucus Callinicus (reigned from 246-225 BC), the king of the north in Syria. During these events Israel is in the so called inter-testament period and is under the rule and authority of the Ptolemaic dynasty.

[9] So the king of the south shall come into his kingdom, and shall return into his own land.

Ptolemy Euergetes did not stop at Syria but attempted to overthrow the entire Seleucid dynasty by taking land beyond the Euphrates River and westward into Asia Minor. An act of treason at his home base in Egypt apparently prevented him from conquering the entire Seleucid territory.

[10] But his sons shall be stirred up, and shall assemble a multitude of great forces: and one shall certainly come, and overflow, and pass through: then shall he return, and be stirred up, even to his fortress.

The descendants and heirs to the Seleucid throne will react to the invasion of the Ptolemy dynasty from the south by attempting to regain their birthright and domain. Putting themselves at the head of a great host, one of the sons unexpectedly dies from falling from his horse in battle. History has shown this to be the son of Callinicus, Seleucus. Therefore, the prophecy tells us that one, not two, of the sons "shall certainly come…" This is the other son of Callinicus, Antiochus III, who regained much of the territory lost to Ptolemy

Euergetes, including Israel which would now be under Seleucid rule. According to Strabo, he returned to Syria, likely in winter time, and Antiochus III waited till "the time that kings go out to battle" (1 Chronicles 20:1) that is in the spring time, and attacked "his fortress" that is the fortress of the son of Ptolemy Euergetes, Ptolemy IV Philopater (reigned 221-205 BC) in 217 BC, meaning the fortress of the Ptolemic dynasty in Raphia or Gaza on the border of Israel and Egypt.

[11] And the king of the south shall be moved with choler, and shall come forth and fight with him, even with the king of the north: and he shall set forth a great multitude; but the multitude shall be given into his hand.

Because of the brazen attack by Antiochus III at the border of the Ptolemaic homeland, the king of the south being ironically named Ptolemy IV Philopater (he murdered his father Euergetes) battled the king of the north (Antiochus III) at Gaza or Raphia. According to Polybius the Greek historian whose work *The Histories* covers 264-146 BC, the great multitude set up by Philopater consisted of 70,000-foot soldiers, 5,000 horses, and seventy-three elephants. Not to be outdone, Antiochus III arrayed an army of 72,000-foot soldiers, 6,000 horses, and 102 elephants. Although outnumbered, the king of the south, Philopater, defeated Antiochus III, pushed him back from their border and slew 10,000 soldiers, 300 horsemen, and 4,000 prisoners of war.

[12] And when he hath taken away the multitude, his heart shall be lifted up; and he shall cast down many ten thousands: but he shall not be strengthened by it.

According to 3 Maccabees, Philopater upon pushing back the Seleucids visited the cities and temples of the regions in and around Israel. Upon his admiration of the Temple in Jerusalem he did not hearken unto the priests and inhabitants and attempted to enter into the Holy of Holies but was smitten by God and "paralyzed in his limbs and unable to speak." Eventually Philopater recovered but did not forget and continued to breathe out violent threats against the Jews and their God (3 Maccabees 1-2). Nevertheless, upon victory "he shall not be strengthened" that is to say Philopater did not pursue Antiochus III and thereby terminate any future revenge.

[13] For the king of the north shall return, and shall set forth a multitude greater than the former, and shall certainly come after certain years with a great army and with much riches.

After a 14-year interval and upon licking his wounds and restocking his army, Antiochus III (reigned 222-187 BC) once again invaded Egypt upon the death of Philopater (205 BC) and during the reign of his son Ptolemy V Epiphanes (204-181 BC) who was installed as Pharaoh at five years old.

[14] And in those times there shall many stand up against the king of the south: also the robbers of thy people shall exalt themselves to establish the vision; but they shall fall.

Sensing the weakness of the Ptolemy dynasty under the rule of a five-year-old (obviously assisted by the administration) Antiochus III made a pact with Phillip the king of Macedon and therefore "many stood up against the king of the south" and invaded Egypt and divide the region between the two powers with an army of 300,000-foot soldiers and the previously mentioned "much riches" were the desperately needed supplies to keep the massive army marching. The phrase "also the robbers of *thy* people…" is directed towards Daniel and more specifically the nation of Israel during this future period. These Jewish robbers would apparently take advantage of the chaotic state of Egypt by crossing the border of Israel to plunder Egyptian goods or possibly it could mean that while Israel was in disarray during the battles of the Seleucid and Ptolemic dynasties they would take advantage of their own countrymen. Many of these Jews upon the victory of Philopater at Gaza in 217 BC sided with the Pharaoh and became converts to the Greek religion. Nevertheless, upon the region falling back into the hands of Antiochus III 14 years later, Antiochus III destroyed the traitors.

[15] So the king of the north shall come, and cast up a mount, and take the most fenced cities: and the arms of the south shall not withstand, neither his chosen people, neither shall there be any strength to withstand.

Antiochus III, king of Syria, having conquered Egypt with the assistance of Phillip of Macedon, now takes the walled cities in the yet conquered remaining territory of the broken Ptolemic dynasty.

[16] But he that cometh against him shall do according to his own will, and none shall stand before him: and he shall stand in the glorious land, which by his hand shall be consumed.

History tells us that the dynasty in Egypt could not withstand the onslaught of Antiochus III and the cities taken by the Seleucids were in the region of biblical Phoenicia, Samaria, and Judea. Josephus relates that the Jews willfully submitted to Antiochus III and invited him into their capital city of Jerusalem; hence "he shall stand in the glorious land." The prophecy also mentions that upon the march from the north the Seleucid army would consume the land of Israel. Since the nation of Israel willfully submitted to Antiochus III this could refer to the invading army stripping the land of all the food stuffs.

[17] He shall also set his face to enter with the strength of his whole kingdom, and upright ones with him; thus shall he do: and he shall give him the daughter of women, corrupting her: but she shall not stand on his side, neither be for him.

Antiochus III will invade Israel with the full force of his kingdom and then "set his face to enter with the strength of his whole kingdom" that is to say, set his mind and army on invading Egypt along with a contingent of Jewish men now loyal to the Seleucid dynasty. Antiochus III was favored much by the Jews for his many favorable policies such as permitting 2000 Jewish families to resettle in Lydia and Phrygia from Babylonia. Apparently, Antiochus III was unable to take Egypt by military force (which was ruled at that time by Ptolemy XII Auletes) because the region was under the auspices of the up-and-coming Roman Empire. Nevertheless, Ptolemy XII still apparently made a treaty with Antiochus III by proposing a political marriage, giving his daughter, the famous Cleopatra, to the Seleucid king. Nevertheless "she shall not stand on his side, neither be for him" that is to say, Cleopatra being married defied her father and Antiochus III and under the radar sent ambassadors to Rome congratulating them on their expanding empire and seeking their help.

[18] After this shall he turn his face unto the isles, and shall take many: but a prince for his own behalf shall cause the reproach offered by him to cease; without his own reproach he shall cause it to turn upon him.

Upon the public humiliation heaped upon Antiochus III by Cleopatra rejecting his hand in marriage, in a rage he set out to attack the Greek isles which were under the auspices of the Roman Empire such as Rhodes. Therefore, the insulted Roman army and navy drove Antiochus III back to Syria, gobbling up some of the Seleucid territory in the process. An example would be Lucius Scipio who drove the army of Antiochus III out of Asia Minor.

[19] Then he shall turn his face toward the fort of his own land: but he shall stumble and fall, and not be found.

Being in retreat from the threatening Roman forces, Antiochus III returned to his capital at Antioch, the "fort of his own land." Having an empty war chest and also needing to repay his debtors, Antiochus III and a band of his men attempted to invade the treasury of the Temple of Elymaeus in 187 BC in the region of Persia, but when the locals discovered the thievery they slew Antiochus the Great.

[20] Then shall stand up in his estate a raiser of taxes in the glory of the kingdom: but within few days he shall be destroyed, neither in anger, nor in battle.

Upon the heels of the death of Antiochus III (The Great) his son Seleucus Philopater IV (reigned 187-175 BC) stood up in his father's place to rule the dynasty and subsequently raise taxes yearly in order to fill the war chest and pay back their loans to the Roman Empire. 2 Maccabees mentions the government appointed tax collector Heliodorus coming to Jerusalem to collect taxes (2 Maccabees 3:7). The mention of the king's untimely death is confirmed in history as the same Heliodorus poisoned the king in an act of sedition likely at the bidding of the up-and-coming monster of iniquity, Antiochus Epiphanes IV.

[21] And in his estate shall stand up a vile person, to whom they shall not give the honour of the kingdom: but he shall come in peaceably, and obtain the kingdom by flatteries.

Upon the death of Seleucus Philopater IV, his brother, Antiochus Epiphanes IV, came upon the political scene. The "vile person" was notorious for his many vices such as lewdness, drunkenness, and fornication, and took upon himself the nickname "Epiphanes," which means "illustrious," the opposite of his character, while his adversaries in a word play called him "Epimanes" meaning mad man. But "they shall not give the honor of the kingdom" to Epiphanes, that is to say the ruling elite in the Seleucid dynasty knowing his history of behavior in his twelve-year Roman imprisonment were reluctant to appoint him king. Nevertheless, he came in peacefully and obtained the kingdom, that is to say, he pretended to take the kingdom for his nephew Demetrius who was imprisoned in Rome so that there was no opposition. But once he secured the dynasty for his nephew, he, through bribes and promises to the ruling elite, slithered his way into the role of king.

[22] And with the arms of a flood shall they be overflown from before him, and shall be broken; yea, also the prince of the covenant.

Oftentimes in Scripture a flood can be representative for a military force (Jeremiah 46:7, Revelation 12:15) as it is in this case. History tells us that parties favorable to Antiochus joined with him in overthrowing Heliodorus, the assassin of his brother, thus removing all in-house opposition and paving the way for his rule and reign. "The prince of the covenant" should probably be identified with Onias, the high priest of Jerusalem.

[23] And after the league made with him he shall work deceitfully: for he shall come up, and shall become strong with a small people.

"The league made with him" is likely referring to the promises made by Antiochus IV that he was retaining the Seleucid kingdom until his nephew Demetrius was released from imprisonment in Rome, but as previously mentioned Antiochus IV reneges on the arrangement and through deceit and gifts kidnaps the kingdom and with just a handful of advisors and soldiers positions himself in line to rule.

[24] He shall enter peaceably even upon the fattest places of the province; and he shall do that which his fathers have not done, nor his fathers' fathers; he shall scatter among them the prey, and spoil, and riches: yea, and he shall forecast his devices against the strong holds, even for a time.

Through political wit Antiochus Epiphanes IV enters and overcomes regions not privy to his background of deceitfully obtaining the throne and which were abundant with natural resources. Antiochus IV is distinguished from all previous rulers in the history of the Greek Empire because of his stunning success in conquering Egypt. The riches obtained from the fattest places of the province were then likely dispersed among his followers, the previously mentioned "small people." 1 Maccabees likewise states; "He (Antiochus Epiphanes IV) feared that he should not be able to bear the charges any longer, nor to have such gifts to give so liberally as he did before: for he had abounded above the kings that were before him" (1 Maccabees 3:30). Indeed, Antiochus Epiphanes IV planned and overtook the Egyptian strongholds such as Pelusium in the eastern Nile Delta (likely the Biblical city Sin in Ezekiel 30:15).

[25] And he shall stir up his power and his courage against the king of the south with a great army; and the king of the south shall be stirred up to battle with a very great and mighty army; but he shall not stand: for they shall forecast devices against him.

The king of the south in this context is Ptolemy Philometor VI (reigned 180-145 BC) who heard the reports of the impending invasion and gathered a great host to defend his homeland. Nevertheless, once again history confirms the prophecy and Antiochus Epiphanes IV was victorious and conquered all of Egypt including the previously mentioned "strongholds" but hesitated to attack Alexandria, likely because of their connections with the Roman Empire (1 Maccabees).

[26] Yea, they that feed of the portion of his meat shall destroy him, and his army shall overflow: and many shall fall down slain.

Antiochus IV "forecasted devices against him," that is to say Philometor VI. It is not that Philometor VI did not have enough military resources, but Antiochus persuaded the commanders of Philometor VI to commit treason and hence "they that feed of the portion of his (Philometor VI) meat shall destroy him." In like manner "his army" that is to say, the army of Antiochus IV, will destroy the Ptolemy dynasty in Egypt. Daniel is here told that "many shall fall down slain"; this prophecy was fulfilled and recorded in 1 Maccabees; "and made war against Ptolemy king of Egypt: but Ptolemy was afraid of him, and fled; and many were wounded to death. Thus they (Seleucids) got the strong cities in the land of Egypt and he (Antiochus IV) took the spoils thereof" (1 Maccabees 1:18-19).

[27] And both these kings' hearts shall be to do mischief, and they shall speak lies at one table; but it shall not prosper: for yet the end shall be at the time appointed.

The two kings referred to are Antiochus Epiphanes IV and Philometor VI. Philometor VI was likely in custody of the conquering Seleucid dynasty, yet both continued to subvert one another. The two kings met at Memphis to have a summit on the future of their dynasties over lunch and apparently came to terms on policies but their pact of lies did not last. Nevertheless, the end of these kings and their dynasties were fixed by the hand of God.

[28] Then shall he return into his land with great riches; and his heart shall be against the holy covenant; and he shall do exploits, and return to his own land.

After his summit with Philometor VI, and hearing the rumors coming out of Israel, the heart of Antiochus IV was so hardened that he despised "the holy covenant," not the pact he just made with Philometor VI, but the covenant between the Jews and the Most High God because they were a peculiar people having a strange thought and practice. More specifically, his disdain for Israel was a false rumor which was circulating among the Jews that Antiochus IV was dead and Jason took the opportunity to seize his position back from Menelaus which was "appointed" by the Seleucid dynasty which Antiochus considered an affront on his authority (2 Maccabees 5:5-11). This apparent sedition caused Antiochus IV in 169 BC to "do exploits," that is to say, he executed 80,000 Jews, looted the Temple treasury, and defiled the Holy of Holies with the assistance of Menelaus and then "returned into his land with great riches" to his home base of Antioch.

[29] At the time appointed he shall return, and come toward the south; but it shall not be as the former, or as the latter.

This is the third wave of Seleucid attacks upon the failing Ptolemy dynasty in Egypt. What caused this attack was Antiochus IV apparently honoring the deposed brother of Ptolemy Philometer VI, Ptolemy Physcon VII being crowned king, but in reality, he attempted to use the occasion to confiscate the weakened kingdom for himself. "But it shall not be as the former, or as the latter," that is to say the third wave into Egypt was not successful for Antiochus IV.

[30] For the ships of Chittim shall come against him: therefore he shall be grieved, and return, and have indignation against the holy covenant: so shall he do; he shall even return, and have intelligence with them that forsake the holy covenant.

The reason the third wave was not successful is given here, "the ships of Chittim (Rome)" came against Antiochus IV in defense of the Ptolemy dynasty. When Antiochus IV was met by the Roman Generals at Eleusis near Alexandria they demanded he withdraw his army from Egypt. In disgust Antiochus IV vented his wrath against "the holy covenant," that is to say, the Jews, and 1 Maccabees states "he (Antiochus IV) fell suddenly upon the city (Jerusalem) and smote it very sore, and destroyed much people of Israel" (1 Maccabees 1:30). The prophecy continues that Antiochus would "have intelligence" with apostate Jews. These converts to Hellenism were the eyes and ears of Antiochus IV in Jerusalem. I Maccabbes states "and made themselves uncircumcised, and forsook the holy covenant, and joined themselves to the heathen (Seleucids), and were sold (bought off) to do mischief" (1 Maccabees 1:15 also see 1 Maccabees 1:43-45).

[31] And arms shall stand on his part, and they shall pollute the sanctuary of strength, and shall take away the daily sacrifice, and they shall place the abomination that maketh desolate.

"And arms shall stand on his part" means Antiochus sent heavily equipped military units into the region of Judea and the capital city of Jerusalem. They polluted the city and the Temple according to Maccabees by committing fornication with harlots in the holy places, erecting a statue to Zeus in the holy place, and offering the blood of a pig on the holy altar (1 Maccabees 1:46-17 and 2 Maccabees 6:4-5). The ancient evening and morning sacrifices were put to a stop by a decree from Antiochus IV, who also changed the name of the Temple to "the Temple of Jupiter Olympius" (2 Maccabees 6:2) and committed the abomination of desolation by erecting a statue of Zeus (Jupiter to the Romans) with the features of Antiochus IV in the holy of holies, thereby proclaiming himself as a god-man. Obviously, Antiochus IV, the little horn, is a type of the future beast or antichrist who will commit the same blasphemous violations in the future Jewish Temple in the tribulation period (Revelation 13:11-15).

[32] And such as do wickedly against the covenant shall he corrupt by flatteries: but the people that do know their God shall be strong, and do exploits.

The blasphemy committed by Antiochus IV will be executed through the assistance of the previously mentioned Jews who corroborate with the Seleucid dynasty such as Jason the High Priest, as Maccabees states "now such was the height of Greek fashions, and increase of heathenish manners, through the exceeding profaneness of Jason, that ungodly wretch, and no high priest" (2 Maccabees 4:13). Nevertheless, there was still a remnant who "knew their God" and were strong. According to Maccabees these are they who "put to death certain women (Jewish), that had caused their children to be circumcised and they hanged their infants…wherefore the rather to die, that they might not be defiled with meats, and that they might not profane the holy covenant" (1 Maccabees 1:60-63).

[33] And they that understand among the people shall instruct many: yet they shall fall by the sword, and by flame, by captivity, and by spoil, many days.

Those Jews who did cling to YHWH and understood their Torah were raised up in this time of deep apostasy to teach their fellow Jews what the Scriptures taught they should do and to abstain from any form of Hellenism. Maccabees gives us an example of such a saint; "Eleazar one of the principal scribes, an aged man, and of a well-favored countenance, was constrained to open his mouth, and to eat swine's flesh" (2 Maccabees 6:18). Nevertheless the teachers and the students would fall by the sword of Antiochus IV, were burnt alive "and other that had run together into caves nearby to keep the Sabbath day secretly, being discovered by Phillip, were all burnt together…" (2 Maccabees 6:11), sold into slavery "and he (Antiochus IV)…commanded them to slay all those that were in their best age, and to sell the women and the younger sort" (2 Maccabees 5:24), and their spoil taken, that is to say, their house were rifled for "many days." Josephus assigns this period to 42 months or times, time and half a time, another obvious parallel between Antiochus IV and the future beast (Revelation 12:5).

[34] Now when they shall fall, they shall be helpen with a little help: but many shall cleave to them with flatteries.

In the midst of total despair, the nation will be "helped with a little help"; this occurred when Mattathias, a priest of Modin, and his five sons, who are known as the Maccabees for a short time eased the suffering of the Seleucid dynasty through military sorties, etc. but were not able to return the land of Israel to its former glory. In this midst of the success of the Maccabean revolt "many cleaved to them with flatteries" that is to say, "the captains of the garrisons heard of the valiant acts and warlike deeds which they (the Maccabbes) had done. Wherefore they said, let us also get us a name, and go fight against the heathen (Seleucids) that are round about us" (1 Maccabbes 5:56-57).

[35] And some of them of understanding shall fall, to try them, and to purge, and to make them white, even to the time of the end: because it is yet for a time appointed.

In the midst of the Maccabean revolt some of them will "fall" not away from the Torah of their God, but shall be slain by the Seleucids. Nevertheless, this persecution will purify those Jews, taking away their garments spotted by their flesh and giving them garments which are white and clean at the end time of this persecution which was fixed by God. Once again, the parallels between the future tribulation period of the Jews and this 2nd century BC persecution are startling. Those who survive the future tribulation of the beast will also be "clothed in fine linen, white and clean" (Revelation 19:8) after a tribulation of three and a half years.

[36] And the king shall do according to his will; and he shall exalt himself, and magnify himself above every god, and shall speak marvellous things against the God of gods, and shall prosper till the indignation be accomplished: for that that is determined shall be done.

Some understand this king to be Antiochus Epiphanes IV, who prospered in his office and expanded his might at will. Yet on a second look Antiochus IV could not "do according to his will" because his limitations and ambitions were bound in the declining Greek Empire and by the up-and-coming legs of iron, the Roman Empire. Furthermore, the preceding verses in this account make it impossible for the main character to be Antiochus Epiphanes IV. This enigmatic and unnamed king is identified by Paul who quotes this verse as the future beast or antichrist (2 Thessalonians 2:4). This "little horn" will speak marvelous things against God by "shewing himself that he is God." He will prosper till the "indignation be accomplished," that is likely meant to be understood as the Jewish nation's rejection of Jesus as their Messiah and their national regeneration (Zechariah 12:10). "For that that is determined shall be done," means the purposes of the future of the nation of Israel under the persecution of the antichrist. This verse starts the beginning of the 70th and final week previously mentioned.

[37] Neither shall he regard the God of his fathers, nor the desire of women, nor regard any god: for he shall magnify himself above all.

The future ruler, coming from a gentile Roman background (Daniel 9:26) will disregard the religion of his forefathers, possibly Christianity. Also, this future leader out of the revived Roman Empire will not marry and will likely forbid his priests to marry as well. Paul prophesies that "forbidding to marry" is part and parcel of the departing of the faith which ushers in the latter times (1 Timothy 4:3). The coming king will not show admiration for any authority or king, but will "exalt himself" (2 Thessalonians 2:4).

[38] But in his estate shall he honour the God of forces: and a god whom his fathers knew not shall he honour with gold, and silver, and with precious stones, and pleasant things.

But instead the antichrist will worship the God of "forces" or towers (*maòwz*). It is likely inferring that the beast will worship the "saints." Ancient sources such as St. Basil's (the Byzantine bishop in Caesarea) *Oration of the Forty Martyrs* states the venerated saints were "they who obtaining our country, like certain towers, afforded us a refuge against the incursion of enemies…and may God keep the 'church' unmoved, and fortified with great towers of martyrs." The God of "towers," very possibly venerated saints of the Catholic church, will now replace the true mediator between God and Man, the Lord Jesus (1 Timothy 2:4). The God his ancestors knew was not honored with a wafer, wine, and a whispering priest. This "god" will be honored with treasures analogous to those gaudy objects visible in the procession of a Catholic mass.

[39] Thus shall he do in the most strong holds with a strange god, whom he shall acknowledge and increase with glory: and he shall cause them to rule over many, and shall divide the land for gain.

The beast will participate in this departing from the faith of his ancestors and will permit it to function in the strong holds of *maòwz*; that is to say, in the temples and churches where this departing of the true religion is carried out and where people commit gross idolatry by bowing down and kissing images of these towers or "saints." The beast and his system will increase with glory, and his "departed saints or towers" will rule over many, such as St. George over England, St. Andrew over Scotland, St. Patrick over Ireland, etc. and the land he and his system rule will pay him with financial gain.

[40] And at the time of the end shall the king of the south push at him: and the king of the north shall come against him like a whirlwind, with chariots, and with horsemen, and with many ships; and he shall enter into the countries, and shall overflow and pass over.

During the height of the antichrist's rule the king of the south (Egypt, but I surmise we should regard this as Muslims) and the king of the north (Syria, but I surmise we should also regard this as Muslims) shall attack him, but the beast shall overflow into the countries under the rule and reign of the kings of the south and north.

[41] He shall enter also into the glorious land, and many countries shall be overthrown: but these shall escape out of his hand, even Edom, and Moab, and the chief of the children of Ammon.

After overflowing into their states, he and his forces will enter Israel, but not Transjordan (fortified by Muslims). Once again history proves that this cannot be Antiochus Epiphanes IV, because he conquered portions of Transjordan including the capital of Moab, Ammon.

[42] He shall stretch forth his hand also upon the countries: and the land of Egypt shall not escape.

Not being able to take Transjordan, he will direct his attention to other "countries" in the region and conquer them, including Egypt. Again, this was not true of Antiochus Epiphanes IV, as once he was expelled from Egypt by the decree of Rome he never entered Egypt again.

[43] But he shall have power over the treasures of gold and of silver, and over all the precious things of Egypt: and the Libyans and the Ethiopians shall be at his steps.

Upon conquering Egypt, he will obtain great riches by force and will, with power, compel Libya and Ethiopia to do his military and political bidding.

[44] But tidings out of the east and out of the north shall trouble him: therefore he shall go forth with great fury to destroy, and utterly to make away many.

In a cryptic fashion news shall come to the antichrist stationed in Africa about political disturbances in the "east and north," likely referring to Israel as it is north and east of Africa, and the following verse indeed place him in the Holy Land. The news propels him and his forces in great anger to destroy the "many" - likely Jews.

[45] And he shall plant the tabernacles of his palace between the seas in the glorious holy mountain; yet he shall come to his end, and none shall help him.

Upon conquering the nation of Israel, the antichrist will set up his tabernacle or tent (the word for tent refers to a military tent of a general or commander). The word for palace probably refers to a royal tent. They are set up between the two seas, obviously referring to the Dead Sea and the Mediterranean Sea and upon the holy mountain, meaning Mt. Zion or Mt. Moriah, the Temple Mount. Yet he shall come to an end, an end previously described as "his body was destroyed, and given to the burning flame" (Daniel 7:11 also see Revelation 19:20). This is the end of the 70th week of Daniel and what is commonly known as the Battle of Armageddon.

Daniel 12

[1] And at that time shall Michael stand up, the great prince which standeth for the children of thy people: and there shall be a time of trouble, such as never was since there was a nation even to that same time: and at that time thy people shall be delivered, every one that shall be found written in the book.

"And at that time," that is to say, the time of future Jewish persecution in the tribulation period described in the previous chapter. There is no age in the history of the nation of Israel that can be compared to their future persecution; not Egypt, not Hitler. Of course, this verse is quoted by the Lord Jesus when he was discussing events that will also take place in this same period, providing further revelation on the horrors to come to the nation that rejected their Messiah (Matthew 24:21). Despite the calamites to come, "thy people," that is to say, Daniel's people, the Jews, shall be delivered when "I will seek to destroy all the nations that come against Jerusalem…and they shall look upon me whom they have pierced and they shall mourn for him" (Zechariah 13:9-10).

[2] And many of them that sleep in the dust of the earth shall awake, some to everlasting life, and some to shame and everlasting contempt.

This is the one and only mention of "everlasting life" in the Hebrew Bible. Multitudes, not all that have perished over the ages, will be bodily resurrected after the time of (Jacob's) trouble and will be judged. In light of the progressive revelation of the Scriptures some have suggested this paraphrase to help clarify the chronology of resurrections in the Scriptures relating to this verse: "and many from among the sleepers of the dust of the earth shall awake; these shall be unto everlasting life; but those, the rest of the sleepers, those who do not awake at this time, shall be unto shame and everlasting contempt."

[3] And they that be wise shall shine as the brightness of the firmament; and they that turn many to righteousness as the stars for ever and ever.

And those that be "wise" or have insight are possibly those who, in the days of the beast, will demonstrate their willingness to understand who the beast is (Revelation 13:18), overcame him by the blood of the lamb (Revelation 12:11), and possibly die for their faith (Revelation 20:4). The "they" mentioned in the second part of the verse that turn many to righteousness in the previously mentioned tribulation period can possibly be the souls saved by the evangelistic work of the 144,000. Jesus, referring to this verse in an eschatological context, states that when the Son of Man comes and "sends forth his angels, and they shall gather out of his kingdom all things that offend…and shall cast them into a furnace of fire…then shall the righteous shine forth as the sun in the kingdom of their father" (Matthew 13:41-43), these righteous are the Jewish believers in Jesus at the end of the 70th week of Daniel that were turned to righteousness and shall like the stars forever.

[4] But thou, O Daniel, shut up the words, and seal the book, even to the time of the end: many shall run to and fro, and knowledge shall be increased.

To shut up the words and seal the book means Daniel was to defend and protect this inspired writing. This does not mean that the prophecies in the book are shut or closed to us, for the Lord Jesus indeed said the reader should understand Daniel (Matthew 24:15). The many that shall run to and fro likely refers in this context to people who are scurrying to resolve important questions about future events based in the book of Daniel, and the knowledge that will increase seems to be that knowledge which is preserved in the book of Daniel that diligent seekers find not only at the end of time (Matthew 24:15). Someone suggested this paraphrase to help clarify; "many shall run to and fro in their desire for knowledge of the last things, and, finding it in Daniel's book, because it will have been preserved to this end, their knowledge shall be increased."

[5] Then I Daniel looked, and, behold, there stood other two, the one on this side of the bank of the river, and the other on that side of the bank of the river.

The author brings us back to the location of the beginning of this long prophecy (starting in Daniel 10:1) where Daniel observes two angels, each standing on one side of the Tigris River and the original messenger hovering above the river to emphasize his supernatural authority (Daniel 12:7).

[6] And one said to the man clothed in linen, which was upon the waters of the river, How long shall it be to the end of these wonders?

One of the two angels now standing on the bank of the river inquired of the man whose body was like beryl and face shined as lightning the time duration until all these things (the events of Daniel 11:36-45) were prophetically fulfilled.

[7] And I heard the man clothed in linen, which was upon the waters of the river, when he held up his right hand and his left hand unto heaven, and sware by him that liveth for ever that it shall be for a time, times, and an half; and when he shall have accomplished to scatter the power of the holy people, all these things shall be finished.

Then the supernatural messenger whose voice was like the sound of a multitude (Daniel 10:6, Revelation 1:15) raised both hands up to heaven to emphasize the gravity of the vow (Genesis 14:22) in the name of "him that liveth forever" (Deuteronomy 32:40 and Revelation 10:5-6) and pronounced the tribulation previously mentioned to last for 42 months, 1260 days, three and half years, or a time, and times, and half a time (Revelation 13:5). The messenger continues his answer to the duration of the time by stating that it will cease as soon as they (the antichrist and his allies) finish shattering the power of the holy people, that is, the Jews during the tribulation period.

[8] And I heard, but I understood not: then said I, O my Lord, what shall be the end of these things?

Daniel doesn't ask how long it shall be, for the angel did in verse six, but instead asks "what will happen to the nation of Israel since they will be delivered from the little horn in the time of tribulation and how will all these events unfold"?

[9] And he said, Go thy way, Daniel: for the words are closed up and sealed till the time of the end.

Telling Daniel to "go his way" is not meant to be understood as Daniel being commanded to physically depart but to cease the discussion. Then a promise is made that the book of Daniel will be preserved throughout time in order that those Jews who experience its fulfillment will have access to the book to be comforted and instructed by it.

[10] Many shall be purified, and made white, and tried; but the wicked shall do wickedly: and none of the wicked shall understand; but the wise shall understand.

The words tried, purged, and made white are also used previously (Daniel 11:35) to describe those Jews who overcame Antiochus Epiphanes IV. In this context, it is referring to those "many" Jews in the yet future tribulation who will overcome the antichrist or little horn. A statement is also made that the wicked will never "understand" the prophetic writings of the God of Israel (1 Corinthians 2:14) but those with insight will.

[11] And from the time that the daily sacrifice shall be taken away, and the abomination that maketh desolate set up, there shall be a thousand two hundred and ninety days.

From the time, the beast causes the nation of Israel to cease their sacrificial program on the Temple Mount and proclaims himself to be God (2 Thessalonians 2:4) is 1290 days. The set number of days given in Daniel and Revelation for the duration of the Great Tribulation is clearly 1260 days. We know the Lord returns 1260 days after the events mentioned in this verse. Therefore the additional one month is obviously connected to the ceasing of the Jewish sacrifices and the abomination of desolation. Some have suggested that, like King Hezekiah who delayed Passover for one month because the priests had not concreted themselves (2 Chronicles 30:2-4), and Judas Maccabaeus, who, with immense efforts cleansed the temple of the abominations of Antiochus Epiphanes IV (1 Maccabees 4:36-51), so the Son of Man will also proclaim a one-month period to cleanse the future Temple from the defilement of the beast.

[12] Blessed is he that waiteth, and cometh to the thousand three hundred and five and thirty days.

The messenger proclaims that there is now 1,335 days or a 75-day interval between the abomination of desolation and "the end." Interestingly there are only two Jewish holidays that have exactly 75 days between them, The Day of Atonement and Hanukkah. To this day religious Jews observe The Day of Atonement as the holiest day of the calendar and look for the coming of the Messiah, as well as celebrating Hanukkah and the cleansing of the Temple which was defiled in 167 BC by Antiochus Epiphanes IV. The future 75-day interval begins with the second coming of Christ or the end of the tribulation and likely takes place on the Day of Atonement. This 75-day period would consist of cleansing the Temple and then celebrating its dedication on Hanukkah and thereby inaugurating the kingdom.

[13] But go thou thy way till the end be: for thou shalt rest, and stand in thy lot at the end of the days.

Daniel is now reassured that he has enough revelation to live and die in peace and that he should be comforted that one day his body will be resurrected. Amen!

Printed in Great Britain
by Amazon